A JEWISH ODYSSEY

In the search for fabulous wisdom, we set off for far destinations – Atlantis, the Indies, Jerusalem. In our pilgrimages we learn we are equal: the Haj requires the same journey and rituals no matter who we are.

In our baptisms (a merging with nature), we are submerged by the same water and on our return what do we find?

The wisdom has not moved.

We were equal before we set off. We were subject to the same forces of nature. So what drives us to make the journeys? Is it fear of standing still? Or is it incredulity at the knowledge that we already possess?

from 'Aphorisms' cited by the Tzadik

Copyrights

No part of this book may be reproduced or transmitted in any form or by any means, electronic or mechanical, including photocopying, recording, or by any information storage and retrieval system, without permission in writing from the copyright owner.

The right of **Ray Kohn** to be identified as the author of this work has been asserted by him in accordance with the Copyright, Designs and Patents Act, 1988.

Text: © Ray Kohn 2024
Cover & Graphics: © Cybermouse Books 2024
Typeset & Layout: © Cybermouse Books 2024
Font: Arial 11pt.

ISBN: 978-1-0687057-4-8

Published by Ray Kohn 2024

The characters in this publication are fictional and any resemblance to real persons, living or dead, is purely coincidental.

In the design of this book, Ray Kohn has made every effort to avoid infringement of any established copyright.

All rights reserved.

CONTENTS

BOOK 1:	THE TZADIK RETURNS	1

THE TZADIK TESTS	5
THE TZADIK REFLECTS	9
THE TZADIK & LANGUAGE	17
THE TZADIK & ISRAEL	25
THE TZADIK & POETRY	31
THE TZADIK AS LISTENER	42
THE TZADIK AS CRITIC	59

BOOK TWO:	BRAZILIAN TALES	79
BOOK THREE:	TALES FROM NOWHERE	121
BOOK FOUR:	INTERLUDE	173
BOOK FIVE:	GREEK HOLIDAY	203
BOOK SIX:	MORE JEWISH TALES UNTOLD	235

PREFACE

Oscar Wilde said the aim of art was to reveal art and conceal the artist. Some readers felt that this was partially achieved in the companion book, 'Jewish Tales Untold'. But this book has completely failed Wilde's test. Illustrated with forty-two short stories, this was my journey driven away from the familiar Tzadik in his unfamiliar guise as a lecturer. These are tales mirroring my travels around the world, an odyssey meeting many different people across alien cultures, until arriving back to an altogether altered home.

If I had paid more attention to his Four Quartets, I would have known what would happen. T.S. Eliot wrote:

"We shall not cease from exploration

And the end of all our exploring

Will be to arrive where we started

And know the place for the first time."

Perhaps it is not the arrival but the traveling which is the point: each represents a timeless moment in the personal voyage. It creates a history. Eliot again: "A people without history is not redeemed from time, for history is a pattern of timeless moments."

So, celebrating each point of arrival and departure, however alien, may be the sole requirement for securing a route back home. I do not know the answer: all I can do is to record the journey through these previously untold tales.

BOOK ONE:

THE TZADIK RETURNS

I was hoping to join a course that claimed it could help aspiring writers with their creativity. I arrived, sceptical, as I doubted that my mediocre ability could be much improved. Imagine my surprise when I found that the Tzadik, whom I had encountered so many times pontificating by the river, standing before the class of thirty students ready to act as a lecturer.

He waited until we had all settled and began: "This first session is an introduction to assess if you would benefit from joining the course. You all have paper, pencils and matchsticks in front of you. I want to set you a couple of puzzles, just to get those brain cells working."

"Place nine dots (3 x 3) on a piece of paper.

```
*   *   *

*   *   *

*   *   *
```

Connect the dots with four straight consecutive lines, without taking your pen off the paper.

I had seen this exercise before, so I already knew how to do it, but others struggled in ways that made me feel superior. After a few minutes, the Tzadik continued:

"Now take the matchsticks laid out on the desks and place six of them into a pattern of 4 equilateral triangles without breaking them."

I recalled that there was no way of accomplishing this in two dimensions: I had to build a 3-dimensional tetrahedron, by making the matchsticks into a pyramid with six sides. Feeling very cocky, I looked at the Tzadik as if daring him to challenge me with something more difficult.

He waited until some of us had finished then pointed to one student, an older man, who had solved the exercises and said, "Mr. Sachs, please show us how to do them."

After a little display by Mr. Sachs, the Tzadik resumed.

"All right. Those puzzles have little to do with creativity. They were just puzzles to get you in the mood for problems that occasionally require thinking outside the parameters that you may have assumed were there when, in fact, they were not. But I want those who solved the problems to sit at the back."

Ten of us moved to the back of the room.

"Now I am going to tell you a story where you will be asked to decide upon the guilt of various characters. This is a different type of exercise and requires you to project yourself into the shoes of the people involved. Are you ready?"

We all nodded, so the Tzadik started:

"A Baron lived in his castle, surrounded by a moat. When he brought his bride home, he told her that no-one was allowed in or out of the castle once night fell. Guards had orders that anyone attempting to break this rule should be killed.

After some months, the Baron's wife became frustrated with the restrictions of castle life. She visited the local town during the day and got to know several people. One afternoon, when the Baron was away, she fell asleep beside her lover, the shopkeeper's son. When she awoke in her lover's house, it was already dark. Knowing that she could not get back into the castle, she asked her lover if she could stay overnight. The young man was afraid of their affair being discovered, so he told her to leave.

She walked down to the boatman's hut and asked if he would take her over the moat. The boatman demanded a fare, but she had no money with her. He told her that ferrying was his living, and he could not take passengers who did not pay.

She walked to the church and asked the priest if he would lend her some money. He asked why and she told him the complete truth. He was scandalised by her behaviour and demanded that she leave the church immediately.

She went to the drawbridge and asked the guard if he would let her pass. He said that his orders were to kill anyone attempting to cross over during the hours of darkness. She tried to rush past him. He cut her down with his sword."

"Now, I want you to consider who was most responsible for the woman's death: and who was the least responsible. Place all six characters in order of responsibility."

We all scribbled our list on a sheet of paper and awaited the Tzadik's pronouncement. Eventually, the Tzadik asked us to hand him our lists and he perused them quickly.

"Now I am going to tell you how I score this." And he rapidly wrote numbers on each of our sheets. "I score you with 3 points if you place the baron on top. I score you with 3 points if you place the wife at the bottom. If you place the lover as the second most responsible, I score you with 2 points, and if the guard is bottom, I score you with 2 points. If the wife or guard is top, I score you with 1 point. I have placed your personal scores at the bottom of each sheet."

He handed the sheets back. I had placed the baron on top (3 points) and the wife at the bottom (3 points) but I got no extra points as my instinctive dislike of the priest placed him second. So, he had given me 6 points. We all awaited his next move and, I must admit, I was a little taken aback.

"If your score was 4 or more, then you are welcome to stay in my class although it will be very much up to you whether you will learn very much. If your score is 1, 2 or 3 then I suggest that you enrol in my class as you may be able to learn more. If your score was zero, I do not believe you will benefit from this class unless you are sitting in the back row – although I can see that all the back row scored more than 4. So, that concludes the initial assessment. I look forward to seeing some of you back here next week, but I do not want to see any of the zero scorers in my class again."

And, with that, the Tzadik walked out leaving us in little doubt as to who should attend his class and who he would not welcome back.

THE TZADIK TESTS

Only twelve of us turned up to the Tzadik's class the following week. He seemed surprised that so many of us had not taken offence at his brusque treatment of fellow attendees the week before: but offered no apologies. Instead, he handed us all a set of questions and said: "you have 20 minutes to think about these four puzzles. Write your suggested solutions beneath each puzzle and do not talk to one another." This is what we had presented:

THE MOON BUGGY

You live in a space station on the Moon with fellow astronauts. The vehicle you have for driving around has large wheels and tyres to deal with the rocky terrain. But with its high centre of gravity, the buggy tips over when on a steep slope. You have no way to modify the buggy's structure but must think of a solution with what you've got.

THE THERMOMETER

You are a member of a medical research team who have discovered that a tiny ant could provide a valuable biochemical. However, to calculate the rate at which the chemical can be produced, it is necessary to discover the initial temperature of the ant. Since a normal thermometer cannot measure the body heat of so tiny a creature, the team ask you to provide them with an effective means by which to measure an ant's temperature.

THE ARROW

You are a technician in a film crew. The crew are getting bored with shooting the same scene repeatedly. It features an archer shooting an arrow onto a target. The director insists that the shot cannot be faked as the camera is placed behind the archer and follows the arrow all the way to the mark. The problem is that the archer has never managed to score a bull's eye. How do you solve the problem and assure a perfect shot every time?

THE MAST

You are a soldier who has placed an aerial on a mast above a hill overlooking an enemy position so that their radio messages can be intercepted. In the cold weather, ice forms on the aerial whose increased weight is too great for the mast, so it breaks. Every time, you have to go up the dangerous hill to replace the mast and aerial. Have you got a solution that will mean you do not keep having to climb the hill?

I regarded these puzzles as irrelevant to the issue of creativity. Just because I could or could not think of ways around the puzzle did not strike me as anything to do with whether I could compose music better, paint more striking pictures or write more interesting stories. But, as the Tzadik had confronted us with these problems, I felt challenged to try to find answers.

Only later did I realise that it was this process of overcoming challenges that he was wanting to assess – not whether we had answers with which he may or may not agree.

My solutions were finished well within the twenty minutes – an achievement of which I was proud. Again, I only realised later that this race against the clock was irrelevant. It was merely a way of ensuring that the Tzadik could conclude the class in time for his dinner.

Once he collected our answers: he spoke about the solutions.

"There is no correct answer. But I shall list responses that would certainly count as solutions to the problems. For the moon buggy, I would suggest filling the tyres with stones to weigh the buggy down. (My answer was to pump water into the tyres). Other answers:

• partially deflating the tyres – but that would reduce the buggy's speed and increase wear and tear

• suspending a weight beneath the buggy – but with the reduced clearance, mobility is reduced

• avoiding steep slopes in the hope that there aren't many on the moon

• pick it up when it falls over as it is so light on the Moon."

I was quite proud of my answer but soon realised that everyone else had solved this puzzle so, if this was a competition, I would not be seen as being in the lead.

"With regard to the thermometer, the only solution of which I am aware is to put lots of ants into a container and measure the temperature with a normal thermometer. What do you all think?"

Most put up their hands to indicate that this is what they had written. I was embarrassed because I had not thought of that.

"Now we come to the arrow. What did you write?" The Tzadik knew that I had come across him many times before: he was addressing me directly.

I said that my experience in filming meant that I would have the arrow shot onto a blank screen and then paint the bull's eye around it afterwards. The Tzadik smiled and I felt vindicated but then he pulled out two other answers from the students and said:

"I preferred this neat solution of making the arrow hollow, fixing a nylon thread to the target, feeding it through the arrow and fixing it just behind the archer. That way every shot will hit the bull's eye."

"The hardest puzzle may have tested you all. Again, the idea of hollowing something may have occurred to you. If you make the mast hollow so that it fills with water in the bad weather, it will turn to ice. This will strengthen the support for the aerial. I can see that your suggestions included:

- using a generator to heat the mast
- erecting three masts to form a tripodal mast

- phoning the enemy and asking their position: if they are as inefficient as most armies, they will simply tell you (I will admit that this is what I suggested).
- signing a peace treaty or surrendering so that climbing the hill will no longer be necessary. (I am unsure who wrote this, but it brought a smile to the Tzadik's face and some laughter across the room)."

The Tzadik started moving towards the door. The twelve of us looked at him, awaiting some sign as to what we were expected to do next. He stopped, looked at us all, and started putting on his coat.

"I am off to eat my dinner now. You are all at liberty to do what you want. If any of you want to continue to attend my course, you are welcome to come again next week. But, truth be told, I have nothing to teach you when it comes to being a creative person. I can weed out those who are hopelessly uncreative: but I cannot do much for creatives themselves like you. If you are creative, you will always find your own way forward. So, I don't really expect you back next week."

And with this Parthian shot, he donned his coat and walked out.

THE TZADIK REFLECTS

The third week was an eye-opener for all sorts of reasons. I arrived, curious as to what the Tzadik would present to us, only to find that, apart from the old music critic, Mr. Sachs, I was alone in the room awaiting his arrival. Perhaps he had cancelled the class and informed

9

everyone except Mr. Sachs and me. Maybe I had missed a communication from him. The start time was reached but still no one else was there so I began walking towards the door to leave. But the Tzadik walked in at that moment. He looked around the classroom and said:

"Oh! It's only you and Hans Sachs today, is it?"

"It looks that way. Do you want to cancel the course?"

"Why? Don't you think you have any more to learn?"

"That's not what I meant. It is just that last week you said you had nothing more to teach the creatives in the room, so perhaps that is why no one else has turned up."

"Perhaps they correctly deduced that I was speaking to them as genuinely creative individuals. Your arrival, however, might imply that you and Sachs are not like them and have much to learn."

I accepted this put-down. It felt like the kind of rebuke that he only reserved for people whom he disliked. It also felt as if he was doing everything in his power to put us off from remaining so that he could go home. I think it may have been to spite him that I sat down and quietly took out my notebook and pen, as if preparing to take notes.

He seemed wrong-footed by this tactic and walked around the room for a minute just to get his thoughts straight. Sachs sat in his usual place at the back of the room saying nothing. Eventually, the Tzadik stood at the front and addressed me.

"I recall that you are a composer. I have listened to some of your work. I cannot say that I am impressed. Much of your music seems to me to be quite derivative. It looks back onto klezmer roots. It uses traditional ensembles like string quartets. You are not the most original musician in my experience. You may innovate, but not create. Do you understand the difference?"

I hesitated – probably more from the shock of discovering that he had heard my music than from figuring out how to answer his query.

"Let me explain," he went on. "Creativity is a process. It might be a thinking process that generates ideas. When you create, you conceive of something original, something quite new. On the other hand, innovation is the practical application and implementation of ideas (usually within an organisational context: like thinking of a new way of making a product). When you innovate, you do or make something that is new. Now: be honest. When you compose a piece of music, how would you best describe what is happening? Are you conceiving something totally original or are you just making something new?"

I had to think about this as it had never occurred to me that my music was unoriginal. Of course, it had strong roots in klezmer as I am a klezmer violinist. I often adopted well-established performance formats, like the string quartet or a violin and piano duet. But I felt uncomfortable with the Tzadik's classifications. After all, surely Beethoven could not be seen as uncreative simply because he composed string quartets, violin sonatas and symphonies which were already established structures within which a composer could express himself? There was something wrong with what he was saying, but I could not put my finger on it.

"I don't think this is helpful." I began. "Did you not start your talk today with a far more significant statement? You said that creativity is a process. Surely, what differentiates a mundane string quartet that I may have composed from a towering masterpiece like one of Beethoven's final quartets is the process that has been traversed by each of us. Mine may have incorporated personal challenges overcome and histories that had become part of me. Beethoven – starting from a pinnacle of accomplishment achieved throughout his previous forty years of composition and performance – incorporated overcoming the tragedy of his deafness as well as the challenges of his practical and spiritual life in 1820s Vienna."

To my astonishment, the Tzadik nodded as if in agreement. He sat down opposite me and spoke as if in a friendly, though serious, conversation.

"Perhaps you are right in thinking that the best way to comprehend creativity, as opposed to other forms of thinking like innovation, is the processes through which creatives go through to achieve something genuinely novel. Let us see if we can identify what comprises the elements of creative thought. Once we understand the significance of each of these elements, we may acquire a handle on comprehending what is unique about creativity."

He settled into his chair and reached into his briefcase. "I have a book here that I would like you to read. It is entitled 'The Act of Creation'. The author, Arthur Koestler, attempts to create a comprehensive, unified theory as to how and why creativity functions. It is a long work, drawing on earlier writing by the same author, and it is difficult to summarise all its arguments. However, the core theory is that all creative activity has the characteristic of bringing together two previously separated notions or frames of reference. Their 'collision' can cause laughter (comedy) or disaster (tragedy). But, most interestingly, it can bring about insight and inspiration.

Koestler argues that all creative activity has this 'bisociative' characteristic. The creation of the printing press is his example where extracting grape juice with a wine press and the use of block prints were two, unconnected processes. However, in the 1450s, Johannes Gutenberg brought these two processes together to create a completely novel way of communicating words. Koestler analyses various ways of thinking throughout the book and demonstrates how bisociation – the bringing together of previously disassociated frames of reference into a new matrix – provides an explanation of why humour makes us laugh, why tragic events make us cry, and why sudden insights make us want to shout out 'eureka!'.

The implication is that bisociative thinking can be generated in an environment that deliberately seeks to bring together different ideas, ways of perceiving and disciplines. These 'collisions' may stimulate humour: they may generate conflict and tragedy. But we might also expect a significantly greater number of creative insights that can bring about new practices, techniques and products. That is certainly the thinking behind how some companies staff their research and development departments, for example."

I had read Koestler's book but said nothing to interrupt the Tzadik in full flow. However, his apparent diversion into talking about how our environment might affect the capacity to be creative intrigued me. I suppose

I had an over-romanticised image of a creative genius in a garret bringing forth astonishing, totally new works of art or scientific breakthroughs. I had not thought how bisociative thinking could be stimulated by bringing together people with different perspectives or disciplines to tackle problems and issues confronting us.

"I cannot believe that Koestler's bisociation is the be all and end all of creative activity," I said. "And I doubt that bringing together various disciplines by mixing people together is some sort of panacea. I was reading Igor Stravinsky's 'Expositions & Developments' in which he is interviewed by the conductor Robert Craft. I wrote out this quote into my notebook. Let me read it to you. "I became conscious of thematic ideas for *Le Sacre du Printemps* immediately after returning to Ustilug." This was his happy Russian home. "Returning to Switzerland... I moved with my family to Clarens.... Almost the entire *Sacre du Printemps* was written in a tiny room... in an eight-feet-by-eight closet.... The whole of *Le Sacre* was completed in a state of exaltation and exhaustion at the beginning of 1912." I would suggest that Stravinsky could not have had anyone sharing his experience in a tiny closet. And no one would deny that the Rite of Spring is a creative masterpiece. But I cannot see how it could be bisociative in the way that Koestler envisions it."

The Tzadik smiled. I think this is the first time I had ever seen him smile! He went on: "You are right. Bisociation is not all that is involved in creative processes. It is one of the elements which may or may not be a significant part of a particular act of creation. But I wonder whether the major breakthroughs in scientific thought taken by Sir Isaac Newton and Albert Einstein were less to do with bisociation and more to do with challenging basic assumptions adopted by those around them and reimagining the world very differently. Creating alternative ways of seeing the world required going through a different process – one where alternative aspects of life could be reflected upon, where various aspects could be brought together (maybe bisociatively, although not necessarily) and this ability to hold conflicting views or concepts and, instead of dismissing what may not seem to fit, allowing them to incubate. This incubation process might be best supported by working within a womblike, very restrictive environment, from which new work could emerge. That would support what you read about Stravinsky's composing the *Sacre du Printemps*."

"Are you saying that incubation, both in terms of the physical environment and through a time where conflicting conceptions can be held before a new way forward can emerge might be just as significant an element as any bisociative act in the creative process?"

"I am sure that that is so. But just as important, although always overlooked by the romanticised image of the artist breaking all the constraints that they may imagine were holding them back, is the imposition of new constraints – the parameters within which mere self-indulgence can be transformed into creative outcome."

"I understand that. So, unless Beethoven adopted the formal structure of a string quartet, his sound imaginings would have remained just that … mere imaginings – dreams."

"Quite so!"

"Oh! I don't feel quite so bad now for having composed string quartets."

The Tzadik laughed as he knew that I was not attempting to place my music alongside the masterworks of Beethoven. I was simply contradicting his original critique of my music that implied lack of originality because it had adopted well-established art forms. But as the hour was nearly up, he was looking to round off this private class by summarising what he believed I may have learnt. Mr. Sachs had remained silent throughout the session, and I had even forgotten that he was there.

"So, elements of creativity seem to involve at least three processes to a greater or lesser extent. There is bisociation, there is incubation, and there is the adoption of constraint parameters within which to accomplish what is novel. There is just one other element about which we have not had time to explore – the degree of connectedness between internally-held ideas and external areas of stimulation around the artist. I suspect that this degree of interconnectedness (and intra-connectedness if there is such a word) is probably also what differentiates living organisms from inorganic material. But that is another area for which we've not time today."

The Tzadik breathed a sigh of relief. He seemed tired. As he departed, he said: "Perhaps next week you and Mr. Sachs might encourage some of your former classmates to attend if you feel you have learnt anything this week."

THE TZADIK AND LANGUAGE

After he had encouraged me to bring others to the next class, I took the Tzadik at his word and rounded up some students. However, those I approached were not at random. I had been wondering about the Tzadik and his relationship with young women. I had seen how many Orthodox rabbis and their like shunned contact with attractive girls. Although he had never spoken about his past, I suspected that the Tzadik had endured an Orthodox upbringing and might find being confronted with a few young women hard to deal with. I know I was being mischievous: but I was also curious as to how he would cope.

As he entered the classroom, the Tzadik looked around and smiled. "I am happy to see you all today," he began. It did not appear that he found young women problematic. Perhaps he was too old to feel attracted; or maybe, I had just completely misjudged the man. All would be revealed during the class – but not in any way that I could have predicted.

"Today we are going to examine the function of language."

Sally, one of the girls whom I knew, an English twenty-two-year-old who was scantily dressed, interrupted and shouted: "we were told that this was a class that could help us as artists."

Just so," the Tzadik continued. "I very much hope that if you attend to what is said today might help you. But only if you practice an art with the intention of engaging others and not merely as a vanity project for yourself."

Sally was quiet, so he continued. "I want you think what happens to you, to your mind, when someone speaks to you. You hear their words but how do you know what they mean?"

Sally called out (now I thought she was being quite rude), "just because we are young women does not mean we've not studied philosophy. Most of us here have read Wittgenstein's 'Philosophical Investigations' as part of a previous set of seminars. We understand what he called 'the language game' so, obviously, any words heard will simply be fitted into the 'game' as we understand it."

If she was expecting Tzadik to react badly to her implied challenge, she was wrong. "I am very pleased that you have studied Wittgenstein," he began. "What he described as the 'game' is what I would define as the constraint parameters within which you have to start to build meaning. But if you believe that that is the only requirement for you to create an understanding of what has been said to you, you are only at the start of your journey. We need to oversee the entire process, the full journey, before we can comprehend what is happening to you as you receive words from another person."

I was starting to feel uncomfortable about having brought these young women to his class. But the Tzadik continued, scarcely pausing for breath. "If more of you had attended last week, you would know that we have already examined how at least three or four elements – in various degrees – characterize creative activity. You are artists and know that there are disciplines within any art form that provide the basis upon which you can build a meaningful creation. What happens when you hear words spoken to you? I would suggest that you are invited to participate in a very basic act of creation – you are creating meaning for the sounds you have heard. You are very bright in calling upon your knowledge of 'the language game' as this is an extremely astute way of describing the constraint parameter you are using when hearing the words.

However, there are two or three other elements that come into play before you can create a meaning of what you have heard. The least important in this case is what has been described as incubation. This is normally a lengthy period within which an artist internalises many of the inputs and experiences prior to creating a work of art. When creating meaning from words in a conversation, however, there is no time for incubation. Instead, the word you hear will clash with your internalised understanding of that word. This clash, which some would call a bisociation, generates a new meaning. Let me give you an example: I say to you (he was pointing at me) 'let's scale this up!' Now my intention was to infer that the basic ideas being expressed in this, and last week's, seminar could be more generally applied to all sorts of situations. But I happen to know that you are a musician, and the word 'scale' will always bring forth other images and notions: just as very different ones would if I were speaking to a mountaineer. So, whenever I say something with meaning A, you will hear it with already internalised sets of meanings associated with that word B, and what may come forth as a shared way forward is likely to be something from both of us – meaning C."

"You are saying that we are all very low-level creatives just by hearing and understanding everyday speech," I intervened.

"Absolutely. But I am inviting you to take one step further and think about what function language is playing. Most people would think of language as a basic signing system. I say, 'turn left' and you drive your car onto the road on the left. I meant A, you heard it as A, and there was no bisociative activity where the instruction needed interpretation. And this is certainly the case for a whole variety of language areas. If I shout 'STOP!', neither of us would welcome a lengthy period of wondering how to interpret the word as a child stepped out in front of the car. But language is far more than a basic signing system. There are whole areas where meaning seems to have been erased though overuse – clichés. If I read yet another story with the line 'fresh as a daisy', I'll close the book and never open it again. Then there are some areas where meaning has faded through age. Let me think of an example … you will not hear people say 'that's beyond the Pale' very often nowadays. If something is 'beyond the Pale' it implies that it is outside normally accepted behaviour. But it is rarely used because the Pale originally described the area around Dublin where, in the thirteenth century, the protection of the Law and the authority of the Crown ruled. So, if something was beyond the Pale, it meant it was happening where no such protections existed. So, language evolves. It is a living embodiment of how we express ourselves. But I would argue, this still misses its most critical function.

Tell me, what do you think most characterizes us as human beings? What has, so far, allowed us as a species to survive whereas most species of which we know have already died out?"

The class was silent for a moment. Even Sally was frowning in an attempt to frame a suitable reply. But the Tzadik did not wait for our answer. "Surely," he said, "we have been able to continuously adapt and reformulate how we live. We are the ultimate artists as creators of our own environment. In our everyday lives, we as a species, are engaged in everyday creative activity. It is the function of language to make us into everyday creatives."

There was a pause as we students took in what we were being asked to comprehend. An important function – maybe the most important function – of language was to invite continual interpretation and reinterpretation of the meaning of words. This was what underpinned our capacity to survive as a species!

Sally broke the silence. "Well, if that is so, I doubt if we've long to survive. We seem to be creating an environment that is rapidly poisoning the planet."

The Tzadik responded immediately. "Of course, there are no guarantees that we will not make serious mistakes. Every artist understands every creation does not hold up under scrutiny."

"You're telling me!" she continued. Sally stood up. She was clearly frustrated by the Tzadik's measured tones. She started shouting; "You sit there pontificating as if you know all the answers. But you're an old man and do not seem to want to face the world as we young people have found it."

The Tzadik's failure to respond to this outburst seemed to aggravate Sally still further. She pointed at him accusingly.

"You're just an academic, a bachelor who knows nothing about the challenges we face nowadays stuck in your ivory tower. What is more," she was shouting even louder now, "you are Jewish so you no doubt support all the killing and destruction that takes place in the name of Israeli self-defence!"

The silence that ensued seemed to go on for a very long time. The Tzadik was not looking at the girl. Instead, he seemed immersed in his own thoughts and was looking at the ground. Eventually he looked up.

"Of course, you are correct in saying that I am Jewish. I was born Jewish, there is nothing I can do about the circumstances of my birth just as there is nothing that you can do about yours. Your attempt to deduce facts about my life from the little evidence that you have demonstrates nothing other than your failure to begin a dialogue with me about my past. If you had done so, I may have admitted to you that my wife has died, and my children live very different lives in various parts of the world. None of them live in Israel and, indeed, I have never visited Israel nor am ever likely to for reasons that may coincide slightly with your prejudices. The fact that Judaism and the State of Israel have become inextricably linked through historical and contemporary events does nothing to clarify the creative roots of the religion. My advice to you, young lady, is to undertake and research more thoroughly any area into which you wish to advance before snatching at conclusions that sound more like the ravings of a conspiracy theorist. They do you no favours as you are, undoubtedly, a far more intelligent and spirited woman than those with whom I have come into conflict and fought in the past."

Because I felt I was partly responsible for this debacle by deliberately inviting this small cadre of young women into the Tzadik's seminar, I decided to intervene.

"Can I ask if full research of any subject is essential before we attempt to create a work of art in that area?"

The Tzadik looked at me. He knew this was a pathetic attempt to calm the situation. He smiled and shook his head.

"As you well know," he was looking straight at me, "you can be an ignorant anti-Semitic moron who exploits all those around him with no regard for their welfare; but you can still compose 'Die Meistersingers', the full Ring cycle and other musical masterpieces. I am sure that Richard Wagner was continually going through all the processes of incubation, bisociation, forming intricate interconnected relationships within his music, and establishing essential musical constraint parameters within which to work irrespective of his evident personality defects.

To continue where I was before being challenged ... just because we are all mini creatives because of the function and use of language does not mean that we are all able to generate outstanding works of art, breakthroughs in mathematics and science or even achieve the ability to make audiences laugh ... a key bisociative activity. These achievements require one other essential element – timing. I don't know if any of you have ever watched old comedy shows. It is very rare that their humour carries over to a new era. Similarly, if Einstein had been living fifty years earlier, it is doubtful that he could have figured out the theory of General Relativity – it was the wrong time. The Newtonian paradigm within which we understood the Universe had not yet reached a breaking point. Similarly, it is strange that what we now recognise as a series of masterpieces, Bach's six Brandenburg concertos, were turned down by their dedicatee in the eighteenth century – they were created before their time!

The degree of connectedness between elements of any work of art may reflect the degree of interconnectedness demonstrated in all living organisms as opposed to the lack of such connectedness in inorganic matter. I suspect that this element is behind the reason why some creations chime with human listeners, viewers or readers. We have not examined how creatives connect their work to what is comprehensible to others at the time. We could spend an entire course discussing how or whether great artists need to relate their output to the world around them, or not. But we've not time for that today."

The Tzadik was beginning to look tired. I strongly suspect that he never had any intention of divulging anything about his life to this class and may have been feeling, in some profound way, violated. It did not take him long to send us on our way and leave before any of us could engage him in further discourse.

THE TZADIK & ISRAEL

The following week saw the Tzadik's class attracting an extraordinary crowd. Having heard from Sally about his apparent dismissal of Israel as a subject for discussion, I sensed that he was going to be confronted with an altogether different set of critics.

Before he could start his talk, the Tzadik was heckled by two young men.

"We want to hear what you think of our achievements in establishing the State of Israel," one of them pronounced. Apart from the skull cap pinned onto his hair, there was no other sign of his being an Orthodox Jew. His friend, however, wore the sidelocks of a practicing Hasid.

"I had not prepared a talk concerning Zionism," he began. "But if you insist on wanting that discussion this week, I am sure I can oblige."

The class members seemed to me to sit further forward as if to give his words a special listening. But this might have been an illusion as the only chair that moved as its sitter sat up with apparently renewed attention was Mr. Sachs behind me.

"So, can I start by asking you which human being strikes you as first establishing some sort of claim for Israel being a Jewish homeland?"

The two men looked at one another and whispered inaudibly to one another. The Hasid seemed content and happy whilst the heckler gesticulated wildly whilst attempting to communicate without any of us hearing what was being said. Eventually, the heckler proclaimed,

"Moses took our people out of Egypt and led us to Israel, fulfilling God's promise!"

The Tzadik nodded. "Well, I cannot tell you what God thought: I am only prepared to discuss human beings as I suspect the Almighty is well beyond my understanding. So, let's look at the notion that dear old Moses provided some sort of claim. I suspect he would have been quite surprised by what you said as he is the only Jew in history specifically debarred from entering Israel by God Himself! It would be fairer to give Joshua the doubtful privilege of bearing this epithet, don't you think?"

There was no response, so the Tzadik continued. "There is one theory that the setting up of the Israeli State was Jews stepping back into history. According to this view, the period of 'Exile' from 70 C.E. to 1948 was when Jews were powerless and had no effect on the course of events. I do not think your hero, Moses, would think much of that description of history. I doubt he would regard thinkers like Maimonides as inconsequential.

What do we think he would make of the rulers and inhabitants of the Promised Land? I suspect he would be more concerned with their conduct than the extent of their power. But if you read Biblical accounts carefully, I think you would conclude that Moses did not have a particularly sound grasp of the problems of political power. His solution to the plight of Jews in Egypt was to flee. And his life seems to have been one great journey – creative and geographical. Building a nation is all about staying put. His interest was all in the Promise – not the Land.

The establishment of every nation requires the application of force in one form or another. And Israel has proved no exception to the rule. But Moses seemed more concerned with the language of ethics. For him, the community is united by the Law which he did not regard as an imposition but as a creation. I think he would want us all to participate in its operation and interpretation. When they built a golden calf, he smashed the tablets not because of their breaking the Law. We all do that from time to time. It was the failure to take possession of the ethics of radical monotheism that angered him. He must have thought; 'If it is not ours, then it is nobody's.' It would just remain as another theory. But if accepted as a shared set of values, then no imposition would be necessary: it simply becomes the guiding principle of Judaism.

Those of you who have been attending these seminars will quickly see that I think of Moses as a true creative. His field was ethics and if we are to study the history of this religion, it is hardly surprising that with Moses' concept of a single, invisible, omniscient, inconceivable Being as the creative force behind the Universe, then we have a people guided by what must be the ultimate abstraction. You cannot get more abstract than omnipresent, omniscient, inconceivable and invisible. I suppose that is why Jews are overrepresented in many of the most abstract fields like mathematics, music – even chess!

But we know that in large communities of people like nation States, it is improbable that a completely shared 'community of values' can ever exist. Our multi-cultural World is the reality, as is the practice of organisng ourselves into nations. The Law, then, and its evolving interpretation is not something in which all can or wish to participate. So, Law becomes either the domain of an élite or, as in the works of one of the greatest Jewish writers of the 20th century, it takes on a life of its own. For Kafka, the Law, like a creature set free, blindly carries out its operational functions unattached to any community, or ethics. The World becomes comical or ironic, farcical or terrifying, surreal or just like some automated nightmare. Terror and bureaucratic control may have been features of Stalinism and Nazism that later contributed to Kafka's grim reputation. But I suspect that Kafka was more in the mold of Moses. His grasp of the importance of Law in Moses' sense allowed him to see a wider secular application to the purely religious sets of rules. Kafka as sociologist and philosopher – more interesting than theologian or journalist. Kafka as ironist and humourist – more effective than psychoanalyst or preacher.

So, when in Europe, we elect Hitler to power and, to popular acclaim, he imposes his Law, it is hardly surprising that Jews decide to set up a State where they believe no Hitler could ever be elected again. Those honest enough to recognise the setting up of a nation state as an act of power are not that interested in justification beyond this. Others are keen to legitimize Israel's creation in terms of religious ideology: and you seem to be calling upon Moses to preside over the pantheon of early Zionists.

But I am sure that Moses would be the first to point out that Israel was not Heaven – nor even a province. As the location where or near where certain people like him did their work, it may have certain evocative attractions.

But essentially, it is just land: and, as such, no more than a place to live or a place to stay en route."

The young Zionist men had kept silent throughout this lengthy, impromptu presentation. But they were unhappy with the Tzadik's dismissal of the significance of the land of Israel as a unifying force in Jewish history. Their challenge to him on this point was turned back on them by asking who had described Israel as so significant. He showed how all writers from Ezra through to Hertzl had political motives in portraying that particular area of land as having special significance for Jewish people.

"I am not saying that Israel is insignificant," he concluded. "I am just unclear as to why you would want to place it as central to Jewish thought. I recall one Professor who believed vehemently in the Jewish tradition of abstract thought as carried by people like Spinoza, Marx, Freud and Einstein being challenged by young men like you two. He was bemoaning what he felt was the failure of Jewish thinkers to have achieved very much in the second half of the twentieth century. A young Zionist challenged him: 'we have dedicated ourselves to work tirelessly to establish the State of Israel' to which he replied, 'you have proved my point exactly!'"

At last, the Hasid quietly spoke. "I accept that the spiritual life is the most critical part of any true religion. Whether Judaism's spirit is entirely encapsulated in the central abstractions that you describe will be a view worth meditating upon. My belief that we are drawn nearer to God through music and dance may or may not sit alongside your account. But for us, living in this century, the significance of the State of Israel and the city of Jerusalem in particular, has become apparent as a coming together of the Biblical promise and the response to the Shoah. I do not think you should underestimate its importance to so many of us."

The Tzadik nodded. "I am sure that you are correct in affirming the significance of Israel for many contemporary Jews, as well as for a broad spectrum of anti-Semites. However, you have joined a series of seminars focused upon the creative process. And whilst it seems to me that your hero, Moses, was a profoundly creative leader in establishing the ethical basis of the Jewish religion (as well as for Christianity and Islam), there seems to me to be very little creative in the establishment of a nation State through force of arms and political arrangements."

"Are you really a Jew if you cannot identify with Israel?"

The Tzadik answered: "My friend, you will learn that you are a Jew if others, especially anti-Semites with power, say you are. Your identity is partially, if not entirely, determined by how others see you. Whether I identify with Israel is largely irrelevant to others who believe that I must."

As the class broke up later, I was intrigued to hear the Chasid trying to persuade his more vocal friend that the Tzadik was not "a wolf in sheep's clothing, a closet anti-Semite' as he was being so denounced. "I suspect he knows more about our religion's fundamentals than any of our political leaders back home," the Chasid said. I wondered how these seminars were going to progress from this contentious point.

THE TZADIK AND POETRY

"Today I would like to leave talk of power and politics and turn to another 'p' – poetry or a more poetic understanding of our languages. I shall, no doubt, draw criticism for sharing my views: but let us see where this takes us."

The students, many more than in the previous weeks, seemed restless. Today they included a Chinese American woman whose age was impossible to determine and her friend, a Kurdish student dressed in army fatigues. The Tzadik paused and waited for them all to settle down before beginning.

"Language may be analogous to games or battles, and clearly does carry a plethora of meaning and symbol. But it is grounded in sound."

The Tzadik paused as if to emphasise the importance of this statement. Then he continued: "As with music, the written word or notation is merely an evolved, visual representation of sound. And underlying these sounds that we feel we control are those that we know that we do not. The sounds of the sea, the wind, thunder, our own pulse, the cries of animals ... these form the vividly patterned backdrop against which we speak. Language, like music, is not written on a blank page (an illusion perhaps created by writers) – it is an endeavour set against a rich world of sound. Some forms draw on this background, mirror it more consciously, and allude to its rhythms. Poetry's sound purveys meaning. Ritual chant and dance are set close to this backdrop. Other forms draw away from this sound world: textbooks, mathematics, dictionaries, maps. Here the emphasis is on visual representation, they may never even be realised in sound. However, when reading a book in silence, the allusion to this sound world is ever present. Indeed, without the tensions created by the endeavour of writing against this backdrop, much of the power in the cadences of fine narrative would be lost. Apollonian artistic enterprise seems rather meaningless unless set in the context of a Dionysian, natural World.

Drawing a line in time is not recognisable as such without the curves and cyclical rhythms that create the matter/material upon which we draw. Language and music are enterprises, and elemental sound provides raw material – uncut building blocks – as well as the noisy background to all we do in speech, song, poetry and prose.

The reaction of those blighted by their language becoming a morass of cliché, falsehoods and deliberate obfuscation is to seek firmer ground, or sink. Sinking is the acceptance of word-meanings produced for mass consumption – the slogans and catch phrases of the day. Firm ground is often sought "higher up" in the visual representations of mathematics and science – a measured step away from the teeming World of sound. The steps are taken in the expectation of being able to retain a relationship with it by being able to describe it in different terms (i.e. not in a language drenched in sound but in terms that attempt to avoid the ambiguities of self-reflection). Other firm ground is sought by trying to "wash away" some of the mud with water freshly drawn from the "natural world". This return to innocence is a constantly-returning tendency in all art: but it is not the classical innocence of Apollonian formalism – that is "higher" ground. It is the unashamed innocence of guiltless sex, dance in a trance, abandoned improvisatory music or storytelling, folk roots.

But the moment that this step towards "innocent" language becomes a direction in which we start to move, the spring becomes muddy. We say one thing, we are understood differently. Language's prismatic qualities re-assert themselves and the search for clearer speech resumes. The problem, of course, is that we appear to find the symbolic power of language so strong that whilst we are in the throes of some collective process of washing away the mud, we cannot help indulging in a spot of "ethnic cleansing" at the same time. Genocide may be our most innocent act."

This deliberately provocative, metaphorical statement seemed to make a few restless again. So, the Tzadik paused awaiting an interruption that never arrived. So, he continued.

"The responsibilities of language usage may be heavier than at first appears. To use the ecological parallel, it may not seem important that we individually burn some rubbish, thus emitting some noxious gas into the atmosphere. The planet is large and will easily absorb it. However, if you are one of many doing the same thing, the knock-on effects may be disastrous – not for the planet that will survive in one form or another – but for you. So, our society adapts and re-adapts around the ebb and flow of language usage. But a concerted abuse of language – the creation of yet another expanse of mud-strewn battle-ground – still leaves a language, for language is large and will absorb our worst efforts. But the effect may be disastrous for you. How can we rescue language, so to speak?"

The pause was not intended to evince a response. It just provided a space within which the Tzadik was able to turn his attention to an allied subject.

"Whereas Buddhism is crucially disinterested in the appearance of time passing, perhaps a central issue in Western culture is to address all questions in the context of time: we seem to be transfixed by the idea of a TimeLine. Whether we track this back to the Jewish concept of history in a monotheistic Universe or Egyptian, Greek or Roman ideas of art and social organisation is not that important. It certainly seems to have a significant impact on our notion of aesthetic beauty: the "fine line" drawn AGAINST the background of chaos. But this visual Universe seems more straightforward, despite its multiplicity of symbolic gestures and signs in colour and form that strike the eye, it comprises a multitude of lines. The Universe of sound has a complexity generated by its effects on the body as a whole, not solely on the ear. It can interact with our biological rhythms – not only the visual or auditory nerves. It can, therefore, transform our basic sense of rhythm and time: poetry and music is more than a "fine line": it also generates its own background.

Spoken language inhabits the Universe of sound. Pulse, resonance and speed affect meaning. Charismatic effects are produced by the way the word is delivered – directly affecting our own body rhythms. Written language is a flight from sensationalism. We are in the simpler visual Universe, here, where the word is a blueprint for meaning, a tool to understanding, a representation of something else. By this, I do not mean some Platonic notion of linguistic meaning. It is just that the written word is the representation of a spoken language (even if, like Latin, it is not spoken now). When the word is written, the pen's strokes reflect social aesthetics and the writer's personality. This is literally the "fine line" in language. In Max Weber's terms, the charismatic personality is expected to become less acceptable as legal-rational forms become the norm: printing and word-processing take over from handwriting. What Weber failed to appreciate was that the written word is only a representation of sound: few people were affected by 'Mein Kampf', millions were affected by Hitler's voice.

So now we pay a great deal of attention to the medium – not just the message. To understand language, we need to comprehend its context – the "game". To discover music, it seems no longer sufficient that we feel its moves: we need to appreciate the context from which the composer writes and musicians play. The artist, presumably, does not paint objects (unless he is a housepainter) but images in the air – reflected and refracted light – or abstractions drawn from such patterns. And it is no good asserting with Buddhist authority that the division between medium and object is merely illusory – that there is a fundamental unity between beauty and our appreciation, between self-expression and communication, between an idea and our grasp. There clearly could have been a radical re-writing of history if, as an accident whilst house painting, Hitler had severed his vocal cords."

The Tzadik looked at the room filled with young students – many of whom seemed to be in thrall to his voice – an irony almost certainly lost on a teacher who had given us all plenty of doubts about how the charismatic effects of a strong speaker could be used by a demagogue.

"I would like to turn, and return, to the matrix of the medium for communication. Each "language" functions through the semblance of time passing (sight and visual change) or through some shared, biological sense of human duration (sound and aural change). Each can simulate a sense of "time standing still" – the statuesque in sight, the silence or repetitious in sound, or the removal of speech from shared meaning in glossolalia. But, finally, our understanding of language is a grasp of the relationship of each to a shared sense of time. I would suggest that the impact of poetry is primarily achieved by the rhythms and cadences ingrained within every line and stanza.

But what else characterises poetry? I want you to think for a moment about the revealing phrase "The mind's eye". When we use language to evoke a response in another person; surely, we can appeal to them by projecting an image within their head? This "image", internally held, is assumed to lie within a special faculty called "imagination". It is not an externally perceived image – indeed, it frequently could never be. So, if you wrote to me ... "just think what it would be like to meet Mozart," I would construct an image for the benefit of my "mind's eye". This image would not be much affected by the sound of your voice – nor by any other physical sound. The sound of Mozart's music, retained in another image-faculty (memory) might influence the image that I construct. Perhaps my aesthetic notions of how such a "picture" should look would affect how I "drew the lines" of this image: probably the memory of a portrait of the composer might be dredged up and slapped on this cerebral canvas. But all these mechanically described operations would take place in a fraction of a second. Indeed, their existence as separable or separate operations seems highly questionable. They appear to me to be more of an extension of the way that we describe mental processes in terms analogous to optics and visually observed events. We know that "the mind's eye" is a metaphor. So are the "images" of the "imagination". They are all within another matrix of meaning – verbal language.

But this is to ignore the fact that when I think of Mozart, I might knowingly think of an image of how he looked. I do not only think of words and sounds. The visual universe cannot be subsumed within language any more than language can be comprehended as an adjunct to optics and art. They may all exist with their own internal dynamics, and with frequently postulated correspondences. But what I am interested in is how we USE and DRAW ON the visual, tactile and aural universes in language; and how such use may fundamentally affect, not just what we understand by such expressions, but the configuration of language itself.

I want to ask you why is language so dominated by visual imagery? The rich universe of smell remains virtually undiscovered and undescribed. It is a universe inhabited by plants and animals and our incursion appears most striking with the emission of chemical pollutants. Is our highest achievement in the olfactory field the production of deodorant? Similarly, the universe of taste seems woefully untouched by language – even French! Outside 'bitter-sweet', it is noticeable how much of the vocabulary is drawn from other senses – e.g. "brandy has a warm taste". This comes from the universe of touch. Considering how significant the tactile field is for human beings as it includes much of our experience of natural forces, violent death and making love, it is astonishing how functional the vocabulary is. Although there is some variation and development beyond the bare minimum, it is surprising how much is described just along the lines of hot/cold, sharp and rough/blunt and smooth, hard/soft, heavy/light and wet/dry. The sound world may receive slightly better coverage as language itself was born there. But if you ask someone to describe a bird call, or a piece of music, the deficiencies of the vocabulary become apparent immediately. There may be some senses of which we are barely aware but that have an impact on the brain. There may be a sense of electrical and magnetic fields that we occasionally stumble over in "a sense of direction". But we have no vocabulary for it – little knowledge of it – perhaps only a bodily sense. In fact, all these senses have a strong bodily impact whilst the visual world does not. Light does not appear to move our whole body, affect its chemistry or shake it up in a way that other media can and do. It is strictly through the eyes – straight to the brain. And language is itself a product of the brain – especially in its written form. It could even be perceived in some Freudian sense as a flight from all these bodily functions. Sound may bridge the bodily and cerebral as a deep chord vibrates every tissue of our bodies whilst sensed in a far more refined way through the ears. So perhaps it gets a better deal from language than, say, touch or smell. But it is the complexities of line, colour, shade, tone and movement for which the vocabulary will do anything. Why is this?

When discussing music, one philosopher found it necessary to view four-part harmony as resonant with 'chain of being' meanings. Now I am not going to repeat Schopenhauer's notions of classifying "upper" and "lower" kingdoms with vegetables at the bottom and human beings at the top (or is it God or gods at the top?). Schopenhauer's tenors and basses do not aspire to be altos and trebles. Language does not "naturally aspire" from the loins to some Apollonian eye-line. It does not aspire anywhere. We just use it; but I am not sure that we always understand what we are using it for. Visual imagery may be the most prominent from the senses, but there is a huge vocabulary apparently unrooted in any senses. Many words describe mental states or processes – cerebral activity reflecting upon itself (e.g. I found it pleasant. He was puzzled. You are intelligent). So, what sort of enterprise are we engaging in when discovering/learning/using/inventing language?

The enterprise may have roots and present uses in interpersonal communication. Our original visual universe was dominated by forests, seas, animals and other people; and they are still important. But the human enterprise of land cultivation, manufacture of tools, clothes, means of transport – and the building of cities – fundamentally affected the content of this visual universe. Similarly, the parallel enterprise of language drew away from its descriptive roots and developed a vocabulary of analysis, explanation and intellectual challenge. These enterprises do, in themselves, imply some rejection of a World that simply revolves, endlessly, in timeless repetitious cycles. Some see the enterprises as "masculine" forms of activity in contrast to the more bodily-orientated senses – "feminine" passivity. Again, it is the use/abuse of language here that gives rise to stereotypical imagery. But this may be a failing of language rather than a blind alley in answering the question. Visual imagery may dominate language because of common goals and histories to each enterprise.

I have read and recited many poems in the past fifty years. I cannot recall many that do not use visual imagery above any other. I find this strangely disturbing as music and poetry have their roots firmly implanted in the sound world. So, as artists – you are all artists here – I ask you to consider what you are doing when you create works of art. Whilst painting and the plastic arts clearly grow from the visual world within which we see: this is not the case for music and poetry. The temptation for poets to emphasise visual analogies may be taking them away from the sound world that they share with music. Language may have become dominated by visual imagery, but I would suggest that the most powerful poetry is grounded in the sound world from which it originated."

The Tzadik, who had been standing and walking up and down, sat himself down. He sighed and said: "I would be interested in any works of art that any of you have created recently. If you would care to leave them for me, then next week, perhaps you can speak about what you have done and give me a break from talking so much."

Then he turned meaningfully at Sally and me, who were sitting together. "Might I have a word with you?"

We looked at one another and remained seated as everyone else left the room.

"You are the only English students in my class. I wonder how much you know about your own extraordinary literary traditions. I do not just mean Chaucer and Shakespeare. Have either of you read Jonathan Swift, Alexander Pope, Joseph Addison – let alone the novelists Jane Austin, Daniel Defoe, Henry Fielding?"

We both admitted that, although we had both read Charles Dickens and later nineteenth and twentieth century English and American novelists, we were only slightly acquainted with these eighteenth-century writers.

"You know, many of them had a sharp political wit in their writings. I would be particularly interested if you two could produce a text with a decidedly political slant. Please feel free to help each other as you already seem very able to plan interventions in this class."

THE TZADIK AS LISTENER

The Tzadik had trumped my foolish attempt to embarrass him by confronting him with pretty girls like Sally. Now he was challenging me to spend time with her (and her with me) to see if we could focus upon creating stories that we would normally write sitting alone. In addition, he wanted to see if we could address contemporary political issues (just as he had been challenged over Zionism). Perhaps, following his lengthy speech concerning the preponderance of visual imagery, he wanted to see if we could take sounds or a sound as central to our texts.

So, I submitted my attempt after hearing the Russian word 'pobeda' on the news (I looked it up and it means 'victory'). Sally, by contrast, wrote about some of the more disgraceful workings of the British establishment of which she and her influential family are very well aware.

I shall reproduce our offerings here: the Tzadik gave us absolutely no feedback. I think he was just making a point at my expense.

I called my story 'Robinson', as we had been asked to remember Daniel Defoe's novels.

ROBINSON

It was a time of indiscriminate killing. I was told about it at school, but I never met a survivor until my first tour with the navy. We were meant to patrol an area of the Pacific Ocean as an exercise that included rapid and random course alterations. We had been maneuvering in erratic zigzag patterns all night when the watch reported a tiny island that did not appear on the maps. The captain, a foreigner whose orders I could not really understand, decided to send four of us on a dinghy to reconnoitre the beach and tiny woodland that almost came down to the water.

Once we were on the sand, we heard someone shuffling behind the tree line. My shipmates immediately adopted a defensive formation as they had been trained to whenever an attack was expected. But the strange man limped out, obviously unarmed, and called to us in English. As I was the most fluent in this language, I was pushed forward to speak with him.

I spent the next hour listening to him while my companions sat without understanding what he was saying. He told me when he was a child, one night the terrible sound of falling concrete woke him. His home had been destroyed by a rocket that killed his mother and sister. His father, who had been at work when it happened, had pulled him out of the wreckage. Soon there were invaders in the streets who shouted a word that sounded like 'pobeda' as they fired their rifles at the people running away. Along with thousands of others who had been deliberately terrorized, the two of them set out in search of safety. Many months passed as they fled through hostile towns and tiny villages where they slept in barns and under hedgerows. As a child he was able to slip into shops to steal food before anyone realised what he was about. He recalled that water was the most valuable and hard-to-access commodity and that his father had almost died of thirst before they reached the coast. But his theft of a flask of tea saved his father although he had nearly been caught by the flask owner – a burly man who had shot at him as he ran off.

Unfortunately, the shot had hit his leg and from that day on, he had walked with a limp. He believed there was something still lodged in his right calf muscle, but he doubted if anything could be done to improve his leg after so many decades.

The other three sailors were getting bored. They wanted to return to the ship, but the stranger was talking without a pause and seemed to want to tell me all about what had happened to him. So, I waved to them to go back and report to the captain and ask for instructions. The stranger stiffened as if suddenly afraid.

"Where are they going?" he asked. I explained that our captain needed to be told that we had found him. "Will your captain want me to board your ship?" he asked.

I shrugged as I did not want to pretend to know what the captain would decide. "The last time there was an attempt to escape the island, it did not end well," he explained.

"My father nursed my bad leg until he thought it would be safest for us to escape on one of the ships docked in the nearby port. But hundreds of others were also trying to escape and only those with money could buy a place. We also had to be careful because some of the men who ran the ships were the same ones who had been firing rockets into our towns and cities. My father made me promise not to tell anyone from where we had come. So, I used the English I had learnt rather than any other language that might have given away from where we had fled."

"Eventually, we smuggled ourselves on board a freighter with no idea where it was going. A week into the sailing, we were discovered and forced to work in the galley. The language spoken by the sailors was strange, but the cooks were kind and fed us scraps. We slept in the larder to keep out of the way of the crew. A storm threw us about one night and the grinding sound of the hull scraping along the rocks terrified even the oldest sailors. As the ship tipped over, the two of us followed the cooks out onto the sloping deck and we slid into the sea. Debris floated all around us from the ship and we clung on. Slowly but surely, it was blown towards the island. The crew nearly all managed to make it to land, but the ship lay on its side with a huge hole ripped down the hull."

"My father and I watched as the crew, ordered by their captain, salvaged what they could and then began to reconstruct a makeshift boat from what they ripped from the ship's structure. I had already begun to search the woods for water and food and could not understand why the crew were not interested in discovering how to survive on the island. Rather than steal food from the ship, I collected berries and fruit that was abundant in the woods and discovered a valuable spring of clear water which I knew would play the most important part in our survival. Even this seemed of little interest to the crew who were dead set on setting sail in the strange boat they had made but which neither my father nor I wanted to board – even if we had been invited."

"The crew seemed to work without any clear plan. Even the friendly cooks kept tripping over one another. My father said it was because they all spoke different languages. The captain babbled angrily but most of the crew appeared just to guess what he might mean. The day they set sail, they left us on the beach watching them navigate their way around the remains of the stricken ship and out into the ocean. We climbed the hill behind the woods to watch the lopsided ship's progress. After a couple of hours, when it had almost reached the horizon, it turned sideways and slowly rolled over. It sank in a minute. We were totally alone, and my father was becoming depressed. I realised because of the words he cried out in his sleep that he dreamt of mother. I am unsure how many days it took him to join her and my sister: but he died one night while I was asleep. The next morning, I found him propped up against a tree with his head drooping down and a huge tear slowly creeping down his cheek. I did not cry; in fact, I have never cried. I covered his body with leaves and carried on doing what he had wanted me to do – surviving no matter what."

"What is your name?" I asked. He smiled and said that his father had told him a story about a man named Robinson Crusoe who had survived on an island. "So, he called me Robinson, and, truthfully, it is probably safest that I cannot recall the name my mother gave me at birth. I just think of myself as Robinson in honour of my father's wish that I should survive whatever problems I might meet."

"How long have you been here, all alone?"

Robinson raised his palms upwards in a gesture that meant he had no idea. But looking at him I guessed his age to be about sixty or seventy. The captain of our ship had received the report from my shipmates and decided to come onto the island himself. He walked over and I saluted him correctly as I knew he detested any slovenly behaviour from the crew.

He studied Robinson carefully. Then, he pulled out a pistol and shot him through the heart, shouting 'pobeda'."

If the Tzadik was intending to introduce some sort of competitive notion between myself and Sally, I think he would have failed as I regard Sally's tale, Odyssey, to be significantly better than my attempt.

ODYSSEY

There was a story that was widely believed in Kabul. Nothing that Khaled later said destroyed the myth of his daring plan. The Taliban checkpoint team were guarding the road and had already killed six members of a platoon sent to clear access for the trucks. The Taliban let locals through on their way to the market. They themselves were all local and knew that preventing access to the market would leave some of their own families starving in the next village. The cart that was said to have been driven by Khaled contained eight heavily armed commandos. Let through like a Trojan horse, the commandos wiped out the Taliban team in seconds, surprise attacking them from behind. The cart driver may have looked like Khaled but, in fact, the over-worked translator was, at that time, several hundred miles away. However, after the Taliban takeover, Khaled was at the top of their list of men whom the new regime regarded as traitors.

Khaled was a well-known interpreter, fluent in six or seven languages and had worked with the British and

American forces. He had received their assurances that he would be brought to safety after the Taliban takeover; but he had yet to learn of the ease with which official assurances can be forgotten and denied. The Trojan Horse tale had pushed him to the top of the Taliban hit list. Zara, his half-English wife, was waiting for him back in London when she was shocked to learn that there were no plans to evacuate her husband. He had spent enough time in London to know that there was little likelihood of a British minister prioritising work to protect a necessarily low-profile foreigner stuck far from the sight and sound of Westminster. So, in a village just south of Kabul, Khaled decided to take matters into his own hands and escape from Afghanistan to make his own way back to Zara.

As a young man, he had lived near the Shah family. Mohammed Shah and Khaled used to go to school together. Khaled spent his free time learning languages and studying whereas Mohammed went into the family business, growing and transporting narcotics. Hoping to walk unnoticed by Taliban police patrols, Khaled made his way to the Shah house. It was a rambling estate with run-down buildings around fields and fronted by a magnificent mansion with elaborately decorated windows and pseudo-Grecian columns. Unable to find his old school friend, Khaled wandered around the estate, unhindered. He tentatively opened the metal side door to the first building and was greeted by the sight of dozens of drugged men and women lying on benches. He felt a tap on his shoulder, turned, and found Mohammed smiling at him. "So, you've found our lotus house," he said. "But I doubt that you've come for a fix like this lot. Come back to the mansion and we'll chat."

It turned out that Mohammed was only too happy to help his childhood friend – provided that Khaled left him a sizeable sum of money. "You won't be needing much cash if we are going to smuggle you over the border." Khaled felt he had no choice but to part with whatever Afghan currency he had to join a regular Shah convoy exporting their highly prized produce into Pakistan. Khaled stayed in the Shah house until the following weekend. He managed to send a single text to Zara telling her he would try to get back to her as soon as he was able. But Internet access was irregular, so he never received any response from his wife.

The convoy passed through the border control without being stopped. The officers had all been well paid by the Shahs to ensure safe passage into Pakistan. But what should have been a routine trade turned into a bloodbath. The Pakistani middlemen to whom the convoy was headed had been hit by a rival gang, intent upon controlling the drugs trade. Khaled's men were met with a hail of bullets as they entered the trading compound. The driver of the vehicle in which Khaled was travelling was killed instantly and Khaled himself was seized on the assumption that he was a member of the Shah family being driven by a chauffeur, and, therefore, could be worth ransoming back to the family.

The leader of the gang was a huge man who wore a patch over one eye. He threw Khaled into a pit and shouted that he would die unless his family paid for his release. Khaled realised that telling the truth and admitting that he was no Shah would mean he was worth nothing to the giant. So, he decided to play along with the charade and wait to see how he might escape.

The heavily armed police squads, headed by the unscrupulous Anthony Asha, had developed an understanding with the traders whom the one-eyed interloper had murdered. Khaled knew nothing about the drugs war being played out while he was left to die in the pit. But after the battle that had raged above him was over, he was discovered by Cirenne, a journalist covering the fallout from the Taliban takeover. Asha knew that good relations with the media were essential for him to retain the façade of respectability under which he operated. So, when she fished Khaled out of the pit and took him to her hotel, Asha told her that Khaled's (and her) safety had only been guaranteed by the courage of his men. Cirenne promised to report it exactly like that.

Khaled was grateful to Cirenne for rescuing him but, as always in this world, suspicious of what she might expect in return. She wanted to heal his wounds, but also to tax him about his experiences. She was surprised when he told her that she shared her name with a well-known musician. The surprise was not the information (that she happened to know anyway) but that he delivered it in her native Italian. Khaled had noticed the Italian newspaper, 'La Stampa', on the table and assumed that the journalist would not have it unless Italian was her native tongue. Cirenne told Khaled that she was flying home in the following week and that he was welcome to accompany her back to Europe. Unfortunately, as all his identity documents had been lost in his escape, he explained that he would not be allowed onto the aircraft.

Cirenne seemed extraordinarily keen to help him. He was blithely unaware that she believed the report of how Khaled had tricked the Taliban patrol. She had begun to invent tales of how he had escaped the Shahs and fooled Asha's men into believing him dead after falling into the hands of the one-eyed drug dealer. She knew there was a great story for which she would be well rewarded by any press owner back home. Her problem was how to get him safely back to Italy with her. She imagined guest television appearances, possible book deals and the handsome Khaled accompanying her on dates that would be photographed by Italian paparazzi. She was determined to get him back home.

Khaled was impressed by Cirenne's furious energy as she talked and bribed her way through the following few days. She had connections that enabled her to navigate between the twin edifices of Pakistani passport control and the Italian Immigration authorities. Khaled knew nothing about how she arranged it but found himself on a flight, armed with what Cirenne called "temporary resident application papers". After changing planes twice on the way, he eventually found himself, arm firmly grasped by his protectress, disembarking in Sicily.

Cirenne settled him into a hotel room in Palermo and took an adjoining room. Each morning, she accompanied him to breakfast before seating him in her room with a microphone and recorder. He wondered why she did not use her i-phone but she said she liked things the way they had always been. "Don't you like traditions?" she asked. At first, Khaled was puzzled by her line of questioning. She obviously wanted to extract as many juicy details as she could squeeze from her captive. One of the "traditions" that she eventually demonstrated was her expectation that he would sleep with his saviour and do her bidding. Khaled complied although it is doubtful that his heart was where the rest of his body was in her bed. But she seemed satisfied – even more by the tales that he had begun to elaborate than his performance between the sheets.

With nothing but false documents and a change of clothes to his name, Khaled did not see how he could escape from Cirenne. He could not even phone his wife as Cirenne did not appear to have a mobile phone he could have nicked. He feared that once she had recorded all his made-up stories, she would discard him and he would end up in an Italian jail or, worse still, be deported back to Afghanistan. He dreamt of Zara crying. He even dreamt of himself as a ghostly Scheherazade awaiting execution if he failed to invent yet another story from his imaginary life. But he recognised that Cirenne's evident infatuation with him had risks if he spoke about his desire to return to his wife. He did not know how she would react so held his tongue and awaited the opportunity to flee.

The occasion of his escape was a theatrical performance by a group of wandering actors and actresses. They were young students and had created a play entitled 'Calypso' which they advertised as 'A Happening' in the nearby town square. Cirenne instructed him to stay in the hotel whilst she flew to Rome to present her editor with his story. She was confident that Khaled would remain where he was as he had no means of escape and appeared content to provide her with all she could want. But he slipped out to watch the play and immediately saw his opportunity to get away. After they had performed, the youngsters made their way to a nearby bar and Khaled quietly joined them. It did not take long before they found themselves entranced by the stranger. Two of the students were Albanians and spoke to one another in their mother tongue. They were astonished when Khaled addressed them in Tosk before he admitted to the entire company that he was reasonably fluent in six, maybe seven, languages. "If you intend to be truly peripatetic troubadours," he told them. "It would be well to have an interpreter travel with you." That night they sailed back to the mainland with Khaled in tow.

Cirenne was livid on her return to Palermo. Such was her self-belief; she could not imagine why Khaled would have wanted to leave. So, she reported to the police that he must have been abducted but could not get far without official documents. The search focused upon the island which gave Khaled all the time he needed to travel out of Italy with his new-found friends. 'Calypso' played in Marseilles, Zurich, Strasburg and Paris. Khaled's French and German – although rusty – was much better than that of his young actors and actresses. He worked as their stage manager and props shifter. They looked at him as a sort of talisman whose presence somehow guaranteed a successful show. But, most importantly for him, he borrowed one of their mobile phones to contact Zara.

To his consternation, Zara reported that the British Home Office was questioning her right to reside in the United Kingdom. Despite showing them evidence of her having lived in London ever since early childhood, they accused her of being an illegal immigrant. Khaled felt more strongly than ever that he had to get back to her. But without any identity documents, he knew there was no way that he could enter the UK legally. His theatrical companions were entitled to visit London with a temporary visa granted to a few travelling artists. But they knew that they would not be able to smuggle him in with them. In Paris, he presented himself to the British embassy, but they did not believe that he had worked with their troops in Afghanistan. The official informed him that he was the third person that week who had made the same claim, just because they could speak a few words of Pashto. He was summarily dismissed and told to go back to Afghanistan "to be with his family". He protested that his wife was in England. But when the officer demanded to know Zara's details, he realised that they might be used as further evidence against her. He imagined an official visit to their home and Zara being told to go and join her husband in France, from where they could be flown back to Kabul.

He wandered around Paris, unwilling to make his presence blight the prospects for his young thespians. The Paris police had started conducting nightly searches to prevent Afghan migrants from sleeping in Villemin Square. He saw that some were housed in cheap hotels and others temporarily sheltered in an unused subway station. He feared that joining them would put him in danger of a French round-up before flying them all back to Kabul. So, he sheltered under a bridge beside a canal. A lame woman told him that she had travelled through Italy and slept in a sewer in Rome before hiding herself in a shipping container heading north. She said she had no idea where it would end up but decided that wherever it was, it would be better than the sewer.

His Calypso companions had been out looking for him. When they found him, he was astonished at their charity and concern for his welfare. He could not thank them enough when they told him that they wanted to give him every chance to see his wife again. They freely gave him a few hundred euros that they had collected at their last performance. With this, Khaled bade them farewell and said he hoped one day to pay them back – perhaps in England. He made his way to the coast where it was not difficult to identify the men who ran the prosperous illegal boat crossings to the English coast. They spoke amongst themselves in Albanian and were caught off guard when Khaled addressed them in Tosk. "How have you learnt our language?" one of them asked. Khaled explained that he was an interpreter reasonably fluent in Greek, Tosk/Albanian, Italian, French, German, English and – of course – Pashto. "I have used many of these languages in my work," he explained. "After leaving university where I studied Greek, I took a year out in the eastern Mediterranean where I worked with Albanians and learnt Tosk." The smugglers were in two minds as to whether they could hold on to Khaled as his languages might be useful with the people with whom they had to deal. But he encouraged them to accept the rest of his money for the chance to get back to his wife.

The crossing was terrifying because the boat was an overcrowded dinghy. It passed within a few hundred yards of a huge cargo ship that seemed oblivious of their presence. They were washed up on the Kent coast where customs officers were awaiting their arrival. But before the officers could get down the beach to them, Khaled pretended to be an innocent holidaymaker caught up in a group of dishevelled foreigners. Putting on his best Oxford English accent, he demanded to know why "these people" were ruining his weekend away. The officers were taken aback by Khaled's assertive demands not to have his enjoyment of the beach spoilt by the sudden arrival of the boat people. The refugees were led away, leaving him on the beach pretending to continue his disturbed walk along the seashore.

With no money or belongings, Khaled wondered how he was going to get back to Zara in London. Once the border officers had taken the refugees away and he was left alone on the beach, he considered his options. He knew that some of the officers might still harbour suspicions about his status. Therefore, he decided to pretend to enjoy a long walk along the beach without being tempted to rush inland. He even pretended to take out a pen and paper (neither of which existed) and sit with his back to any official prying eyes and appear to be writing about what he could see, or poetry, or whatever might fool an officer into believing that he was content to continue to enjoy his holiday after its apparent interruption. Not until evening did Khaled venture off the sand and into town.

A rundown Greek restaurant attracted his attention. He could not imagine that there was much trade for the proprietors but hoped he might scrounge a meal before declaring that he had no money. He did not need to worry. He sat at a table and only saw one other customer. The waiter came and asked him what he wanted. After ordering, he heard the waiter express deep suspicions about him to the couple who obviously owned the place. Taking the bull by the horns, he got up and walked over to the three of them. Speaking in fluent Greek, he told them the truth and begged forgiveness for the temerity he had shown by daring to sit in their restaurant. "I have not eaten for three days and was becoming desperate," he declared. "I will understand if you throw me out or take me to the police. But all I want to do is to get back to my wife in London."

Luckily for Khaled, the couple who owned the cheap restaurant were typically generous Greeks. They took him in and sheltered him for two days whilst he regained his strength and was able to phone Zara. He was keen to work for his meals by washing up and carrying plates and dishes. But they told him not to bother as they already had well established routines which, in truth, he was disrupting – albeit with the best of intentions. So, they simulated gratitude and insisted on paying him for his labour which they knew would be enough to buy a train ticket to London. On the third day, he thanked them and departed accompanied by their smiles and best wishes.

On the train, he reflected upon the selflessness of these unwilling hosts and the genuine affection of the Calypso students. He compared this with the grasping nature of all the others he had encountered on his journey home. He wondered if the police in Rome and Paris and the Border Officers from London were at all affected by the destitution of the mentally and physically injured migrants with whom they dealt. He caught sight of a newspaper headline proclaiming that all those who had sought sanctuary were "scroungers" – easy to attack, defenceless people whom a leading politician seemed keen to regard as punchbags against whom she could demonstrate her pretence of strength. Did the officials see us as human beings, as husbands, wives, sons, and daughters needing protection? Or were we just their meal ticket to a job in rounding up like cattle?

His excitement when he got home was tinged with anxiety. Would Zara be well or exhausted by fear as to his welfare? Would she be worried for her own safety being threatened by the stuck-up government Ministers wanting to appear callous towards dark-skinned people whom their supporters in sleepy villages and towns regarded as interlopers? The door opened and Zara threw her arms around him, then dragged him into their front room. "I have someone who wants to meet you," she said. He nearly fainted when Cirenne appeared. "This journalist says she is writing a story about you and has tracked you back to England. She says she knew you in Italy when you disappeared. She wants to finish her story."

Cirenne seemed very pleased with herself. But Khaled was not at all pleased to see her. But his opinion changed when he discovered that she had given up on the original story that she was selling to her Roman editor. Instead, she had decided that a series of devastating articles about how appallingly the British government were treating those who had helped their troops in Afghanistan would sell better. Better still, she also appeared to have taken a great liking to Zara and so, without any fuss, was happy to leave them alone in their home whilst she slept in a nearby hotel. She had decided that whilst his body was desirable, his story was more profitable."

THE TZADIK AS CRITIC

Sally and I thought we would receive some sort of critique of our texts. But the Tzadik did not even acknowledge them. I felt it was almost a snub as he addressed us all:

"It is extremely difficult to write within the boundaries of a well-known myth. Everyone here probably knows the basic story of Tristan and Isolde, even if you've not gone to see Wagner's opera. In simple terms, the hero Tristan goes to Ireland to ask the hand of Princess Isolde for his uncle, King Mark of Cornwall. On their return the two mistakenly drink a love potion prepared for the king by Isolde's maid, Brangain. So, they fall deeply in love. After many adventures (some accounts include the tragic death of Tristan) Mark marries Isolde.

One of you has ventured into this story and created a new version. I have asked Mr. Sachs to come to the front and read his story to you. We can talk about it afterwards, but meanwhile, please listen to his account."

Sachs sauntered to the front. He looked a little embarrassed at this attention but cleared his throat and began. "My English is not very good. I had a German father, and my mother was Hungarian, an Austro-Hungarian. English is my third language so please excuse any errors of syntax and grammar. This is my story of love and death in six dances. Please attend!"

TRISTAN AND ISOLDE

"They were a very unusual couple. Mark King, slightly stooped as if embarrassed by his height but with an elegant bearing, wore faded clothes that may have been fashionable in a previous decade. Sir Tristan, short with brash clothes that cost a great deal more than they were worth. The two of them were walking from the hotel to the nearby opera house where a celebrated Ballet Company was performing. Tristan had paid for the tickets and the two rooms in the five-star hotel where he always stayed when coming to town. Mark was grateful for his friend's generosity since the decline in his family's fortunes had left him with nothing beyond a ramshackle castle, the aristocratic seat bequeathed to him by his forebears. Although they had spent much time together as teenaged school friends, the only remaining interest they held in common was a love of the ballet."

Sachs straightened his back and made an announcement:

"Here is the first dance entitled 'The performance'."

"It was to be a fateful night out. The audience was packed as the performance of Stravinsky's 'Rite of Spring' had received rave acclaim by critics. The box that Tristan had hired for the season was the closest to the stage. From there, the friends could watch the danced action and oversee the musicians submerged in the orchestra pit. The violence of the score retained its ability to startle the listener; but it was the staged choreography that seemed to mesmerise the friends. They had never seen Yseult Abrams perform before but as the ballerina who danced herself to death, neither could take their eyes off her as her lithe contortions seemed to mirror in every move the rippling sounds that rose from the strings and woodwind. She leapt in response to the brass and shuddered with every stroke of the timpani. At the final curtain call, Mark stammered to his friend that he would do anything to be able to meet this woman.

In her dressing room, Yseult was exhausted. She was looking forward to the drink that her youthful dresser, Josefina, would always prepare for her. This was the final performance of the 'Rite of Spring' and she was looking forward to a few weeks rest. Her twin sister, Jacky, was waiting for her with the promise of a short holiday that she had secretly booked for the two of them. However, before she could reveal her surprise, a knock on the door was answered by Josefina. An enormous bouquet of flowers was handed in that Josefina passed to the dancer. Yseult smiled at the sight of Josefina's pretty, black face peering out through the mass of strongly contrasting white petals. She took the flowers and opened the lavishly decorated card that accompanied the gift. Sighing, she read that it was sent by yet another gentleman admirer who insisted that they meet for a drink after she had changed her clothes. She passed the card to Jacky and asked what answer she should give. Jacky read the card with interest as it was signed by someone she recognised. The name, Sir Tristan, was well-known in the estate agency for which

Jacky worked. He was an exceptionally rich client who held an impressive portfolio of properties to which he frequently added. Yseult said she felt too tired to drink with her admirer. Josefina was ready to steady her with her brew whose pharmaceutical contents were probably not strictly on prescription. So, Jacky offered to take her place.

Even Josefina could not tell the twins apart unless she could see their hair. Yseult wore hers long; Jacky's was cut extremely short. The wig that Jacky wore to impersonate her sister had been acquired by Josefina as a favour to Yseult for just these types of occasion. Jacky promised to report on the admirer once she had investigated his credentials as a ballet-lover and departed with the magnificent wig flowing behind her. On meeting Tristan, she realised that he was smitten with the gorgeous dancer without knowing anything about Yseult. Tristan, although wishing to keep the long-haired beauty to himself, felt obliged to introduce her to his friend, Mark. Although tongue-tied and quaintly old-fashioned, Mark struck Jacky as a more lovable character than his flashy companion.

Tristan revealed that Mark owned an ancient castle that he might have to sell. He told Jacky this to portray his friend as out-of-touch with the modern world as opposed to his credentials as a jet-setting, property-developing whizzkid. He was a little put out when Mark's castle seemed to interest the young woman more than all his boasts of wealth and power. Jacky suggested that all three of them might drive out of the city so that she could see the castle for herself. Even as she spoke, she tried to sound like a breathless girl excited at the prospect of seeing a real castle rather than a shrewd estate agent on the lookout for a prospective sale. They arrived late that night so Mark, being a gentleman, offered Jacky a bedroom set away from where he and Tristan were to sleep. But it came as no surprise to Jacky when Tristan paid her a visit in the middle of the night."

Again, the speaker puffed out his chest like a town crier and announced:

"Here is the second dance: The simulation."

"She had kept her wig on as she half expected him to make an appearance. His clumsy attempts to stimulate Jacky into wanting to dance herself to death (or at least into a passionate embrace) she dealt with by emulating sexual excitement. By the morning, Tristan was fully convinced that he had found the partner with whom he would share the rest of his life. And, in a way, he was right.

Innocent of the goings-on under his roof, Mark showed Jacky around the castle after breakfast. He introduced her to Ahasver, a muscular black Dutchman whose role was to keep some order to the gardens that had once seen better days. She graciously admired the trees and plants although, in truth, it was not these that most interested her. But when he showed her the sparse, draughty rooms, there were unusual features that attracted her professional attention. The Priest's Hole behind the fire in the master bedroom was cunningly hidden. And the oubliette that opened up under the stairwell was operated by a lever that looked like a statue of a hairy goat at the top of the stairwell. She remarked that she had never seen an oubliette before; so, Mark showed her the locked space beneath the stairs into which the enemies of his feudal ancestors could be cast as they rushed up, swords drawn, towards the bedrooms. As she seemed genuinely intrigued, he explained how it could be opened at the top or bottom of the stairs but that it closed automatically with a sprung lever beside the hairy goat.

Although she was attracted towards the modest Mark, she knew that he was really interested in Yseult. Similarly, the randy Tristan believed his intentions were all being directed towards her sister. So, she made her excuses about needing to tidy up affairs at the opera house but promised to be in touch in a day or two. As she left, she noticed that Mark kept a spare set of keys hanging on a hook beside the front door. She returned to her sister by train and felt relief at being able to remove the wig once she was out of sight of the admirers. On the way back, she pictured the keys hanging by the front door. Then, as if from nowhere, an embryonic notion entered her head that she found hard to resist. She was unsure if the idea could become a realistic plan; but by the time the train came to rest at the terminus, it had incubated and taken an irresistible form to which she felt overwhelmingly drawn. She met Yseult and spoke to her about the lovable Mark whose castle she had visited. She told her that Tristan, who had sent the flowers, should be avoided. And she offered to send her on the week's holiday on a canal barge that she had originally planned for the two of them as a present that Yseult could share with Mark. Yseult insisted on meeting Mark herself before she would agree to this; but her sister had already convinced her that the aristocrat would make a convivial partner – at least for a week away.

It proved easy to entice Mark to the holiday riverboat. Yseult had only to pretend that it was she who had visited his castle and the two of them sailed off with Josefina as chaperone and assistant to the barge steersman, Ahasver. By the time the happy party of four returned, Jacky had achieved almost all that she had planned. Even before the barge had started off down the river, she had arranged to meet Tristan. Believing that he was going to meet the dancer whom he had bewitched with his amorous advances, he was only too keen to come to the picturesque cliff top that she suggested. There, in the moonlight, with her long fair wig tickling his neck, he found it hard to resist the caresses she planted all over his body. It was not until he pressed her for still more intimate sexual favours that she demurred. Acting as the innocent ballerina, she told him that she would only be his if they could receive the blessing of a formal marriage. Tristan, who had never received such an invitation before, said he would be happy to marry his wonderful bride as soon as possible."

Sachs stood to announce the third dance, 'The fall'

"The very next day saw the couple wedded in an afternoon civil ceremony attended by no one. As she signed the marriage contract, Jacky's signature puzzled Tristan. She explained that she used Yseult as a stage name and that her real name was Jacky. She also revealed that his friend, Mark, had agreed to let them use his castle as the first stage of their honeymoon trip. Tristan smiled as he felt that his old friend was acknowledging that although they were both drawn to the beautiful dancer, it was the better man who had won the fair lady. Jacky had already acquired the keys to the ancient pile from her estate agency through whom Mark was hoping to sell the place. They drove out to the castle with Tristan becoming increasingly excited at the prospect of a night alone with his bride. She made him wait downstairs until she was ready to receive him. Dressed in revealing lingerie, she called him from the top of the stairs. His descent into the oubliette was followed by a thud as he hit the floor. His cries for help later that night echoed around the empty castle. Jacky had long since departed.

The next day, Jacky quietly returned the castle keys to the key cupboard in the estate agency office. She was sure that no one would want to inspect the property but that, if they did, she was the agent required to show them around. Knowing that Mark would not be back for a week allowed her to speculate that she would soon be a widow. Her sole concern was to establish a reliable alibi for the previous day. To set this up she had driven to a small hotel up the river and registered as a guest on the morning of the marriage. She had told the hotel owners that she was going for a walk in the country and would only be back that night. Setting off in her hiking gear, she hoped that they would provide some cover for her murderous plan. Changing from her gear into more attractive clothes, she had driven her car – parked some distance from the hotel – to meet her bridegroom. After dropping him into the oubliette, she had changed back into her hiking gear and driven back to the hotel. After a restful night, she rose to greet her sister and Mark as the barge parked, as planned, for its breakfast stop at the hotel.

Mark was amazed to meet his sweetheart's twin. Of course, he found no difficulty in seeing their difference: his had long, luscious hair whereas the sister looked as if she had been scalped. Yseult was happy to see her sister and whispered how much she liked the tall, modestly handsome aristocrat. Josefina confirmed that after the previous night's evening meal, both had consumed strong drink and appeared to be happy lying in each other's arms as the barge floated along under the stars. Jacky said she had spent the previous day on her own little hiking holiday and that, after springing her surprise visit to the boating party, she had to return to the city and go back to work. However, she made them promise not to return to the castle but to come to her apartment when they got back at the end of the week as she had another little surprise waiting for them.

The week passed happily for Yseult and Mark. Josefina, who was increasingly attracted to Ahasver, ensured that all the domestic chores were dealt with and was delighted that the dancer whom she so admired may, at last, have found someone whom Josefina felt would make a fine mate. Ahasver had taken them all around the countryside and showed them views they would never have seen from the dry land. On disembarking, Josefina and he decided to go off on their own leaving Yseult and Mark to make their way to Jacky's apartment. She welcomed them but affected great anxiety in her tone of voice. They were excited by their trip and wanted to tell her all about it, but Yseult sensed her sister's mood and asked what was wrong.

She told them that whilst they were away, she had been courted by Mark's friend, Tristan. She repeated for the sake of her sister that the initial impression he had made was not good. However, she had quickly realised that his intentions were honourable, and it was his excitement that had made his headlong rush towards her so off-putting. In the event, he had proposed to her, and they had, in fact, got married on the spur of the moment.

Yseult congratulated her sister. Mark, although surprised at the unusual behaviour of his friend, eyed Yseult and said he hoped Jacky's marriage would be as long and as happy as he would like his to be. It was then that Jacky appeared to break down. She declared that after their wedding in the registry office, Tristan had hurried away to make some arrangements and made her promise to keep their marriage secret and to meet him back at the opera house in two days' time. She said she had no idea why he had chosen the opera house for their rendezvous nor what spectacular honeymoon arrangements Tristan had rushed off to organise. She had faithfully carried out what he requested and had gone off hiking for a day and respected his wish to keep their marriage secret until he could announce it in his own way. She reminded them that she had even met them just a day into their barge trip before returning to meet her husband. But he had never shown up. She had visited the opera house every day but not seen him. She had expected to be able to greet them with her husband with the news of their marriage but, instead, she began to weep saying she did not know what to do.

As she said she had no idea of where he normally lived nor anything about his work, Jacky made a sorry figure who seemed to be throwing herself before Mark as the man who might know about his friend. Mark responded gallantly and explained that Tristan was a very wealthy property developer and that a call to his office might reveal where he had been held up. When this simply confirmed the boss's disappearance, Jacky suggested that if they could go to his house, they might find him hurt. But Mark explained that Tristan owned a very large number of houses and tended to live in hotels. So it was not until the next day that they reported him missing to the police. At Yseult's helpful suggestion, she and Mark travelled to several country houses that Mark knew were owned by Tristan."

Sachs walked across the classroom and made a strange-looking hop saying "Here we have the fourth dance: The leap"

"Jacky said she would return to work and await what the police would find. Unseen, she pocketed the castle key at lunchtime and paid a visit to Mark's deserted home that evening. Unlocking the oubliette, she checked that her husband had expired then, wearing gloves, expertly released the catch at the top of the stairs so that the yawning gap was exposed. Then she twisted the automatic closing lever so that it appeared to have malfunctioned. Taking a run, she leapt acrobatically over the gap and grabbed the banister to prevent her tumbling down the bottom flight. For all the world, it would look as if Tristan had accidently fallen into the oubliette as it had failed to close the last time that Mark had demonstrated it from the bottom of the stairs. Then she took the spare set of keys hanging by the front door and tossed them into the oubliette so it would appear that Tristan had helped himself to them. She returned her castle key when she got back to the office and worked unassumingly for the rest of the day. House buyers were thin on the ground, and it was obvious to all the agents that the office could not support the half dozen employees unless the market picked up soon. So, Jacky was not surprised when the manager asked her and two others to come into his office at the end of the day.

Meeting Yseult and Mark at her apartment that evening, she affected deep despair at still having heard nothing from her husband coupled with news that she had now lost her job. Yseult was sympathetic whilst Mark suggested that she might like a break from the city by accompanying them to his home for the weekend. She agreed with simulated reluctance. As Yseult was not due to perform for another month Josefina had gone off to visit her ageing parents and wayward brothers. It was just the three of them who drove up to the castle the next morning. What they discovered had the police and forensic teams swarming all over the place before lunch.

The inevitable interviews were followed by understandable suspicion falling upon the wife who would inherit Tristan's considerable wealth. However, without any evidence and the testament of the riverside hoteliers swearing that Jacky had been hiking locally (even though they had nor actually accompanied her on her walking trip), it was eventually concluded that Tristan had fallen into the oubliette as a result of the faulty closure mechanism. What he was doing in his friend's home was never established although the sentimental Yseult said she suspected that he had come to prepare a romantic surprise for his bride in his friend's empty castle.

Jacky's plan seemed to be working well but she needed a few months before the second half could be launched. Establishing the size of her huge inheritance took many weeks. Realising a block of cash required selling a few properties that she knew about through her former job. Mark could not bring himself to ask Yseult for her hand in marriage as he was so ashamed to admit that he was almost penniless. However, when Jacky offered to buy the castle for cash, he could hardly refuse the offer. After the sale was completed, she told Mark that he was welcome to remain in his family home for as long as he wished. He was so grateful that he almost forgot about the fate of his friend and the case that the police had only just closed. His proposal of marriage to Yseult was enthusiastically accepted although the wedding would have to wait until she had completed the following month's ballet engagements.

Jacky's plan was based on the adage that solutions to a murder would only be found in the roots of motive, means and opportunity. She had ideas for planting motive for her next victim but had not yet established means and opportunity. One afternoon, however, seeing Josefina and Ahasver walking together beside the potting shed that Ahasver used for gardening brought an instant solution to her problem. Her chuckle was the only sign that she felt a tricky question was now matched with an elegant answer that she had evolved through an impressive combination of logic and creativity. She skipped happily up to the house and suggested to Mark that they should book seats to attend the final night of the forthcoming ballet in which Yseult was, again, the prima ballerina."

Sachs stood and started an odd writhing motion. I thought he was trying (rather pathetically) to emulate a snake. "The fifth dance: Jealousy!"

"It struck Jacky as deeply ironic that Yseult's ballet was a choreographed depiction of Tristan and Isolde to the music of Richard Wagner. Their father had named her sister Yseult because of his fascination with the myth. But it was Jacky's dead husband who had inadvertently given her the surname of Tristan. Now her sister was, in reality, betrothed to Mark – a wedding that she, Mrs Tristan, was determined to subvert – whilst on stage her marriage to King Mark would be foiled by the intrigue and lust of an unconvincing actor playing Tristan. Mark and Jacky watched Yseult's performance with pride. She was a truly remarkable dancer. As Isolde took the love potion from her black maid, Brangain, Jacky smiled at the way that love and death were so intermingled both on stage and off. At the interval, she remarked to Mark how much Brangain resembled Josefina; then, as if thinking aloud, she voiced an aside that at least Brangain on stage was not jealous of her mistress. Mark was curious about this puzzling statement. And like Emilia's handkerchief in Shakespeare's masterpiece about jealousy, the statement sowed the seeds of doubt in Mark King's mind. Jacky pretended that the comment was not important, but this merely heightened Mark's interest in what she meant. Eventually, she simulated a reluctant admission that she knew Josefina was jealous of

Yseult's success. It was important to establish this lie in Mark's mind for the second half of her plan to succeed.

After the final curtain call, Mark and Jacky made their way casually to the backstage. By the time they sauntered up to Yseult's dressing room, she had drunk the brew that Josefina always made for her at the end of the performance. The police identified the toxin that killed her as a cyanide-based weed killer that they also found in the potting shed frequented by Ahasver and Josefina. Ahasver truthfully asserted that he had never seen nor purchased the fatal poison. However, its presence and the apparent motive, means and opportunity for Josefina to kill the dancer was sufficient to have her convicted to life imprisonment a couple of months later.

Devastated by the loss of his friend and his fiancée, Mark needed looking after. Jacky took care of him and, as the weeks went by, he could not fail to notice how she was letting her hair grow long. Little by little, she appeared to him as a reincarnation of her twin. There were occasions when he would inadvertently call her Yseult. By the end of the year, Jacky's plan had succeeded as she not only owned Tristan's wealth and Mark's castle, but she had also obtained Mark as the fiancé on whom she had set her heart from their first meeting.

Sitting alone in prison, Josefina reflected about her situation. She knew that she was innocent of the crime for which she had been convicted. She figured that if she thought long and hard enough, she would be able to work out who was the real murderer. Only Ahasver visited her as everyone else believed in her guilt. It was he who told her about Jacky's transformation as her hair grew longer. It was he who witnessed the peculiar sight of Jacky burning the long, blonde wig beside the potting shed. It was he who first intimated that it was Jacky who had begun to act strangely after she saw him witnessing the garden fire. And he was sure that she had suggested to her gullible husband-to-be that Ahasver should be dismissed and left to drift away from the estate as if he might have seen something embarrassing.

But it was Josefina who began to piece together the suspicious elements of what had been occurring and started talking with her constant visitor as to what might be done to introduce justice. The potting shed was only accessible from the house. Extracting the weed killer that was used on Yseult would have been easy except Ahasver knew that no cyanide-based poisons were ever kept there. Therefore, the discovery of the incriminating liquid meant that someone had planted it. The only people who could have placed it there were Josefina, Ahasver, Mark, Yseult or Jacky. As Mark was besotted with Yseult and due to marry her, Josefina ruled him out as a suspect. She knew that Ahasver had no motive to kill, Yseult had no motive to commit suicide, she herself was innocent which left only Jacky. Then she re-examined all that she knew of the death of Tristan and, like the police before her, saw Jacky as the sole beneficiary.

For many days Josefina lay perplexed in her cell. Then, one night, she had a prophetic dream that she relayed to Ahasver. In it her hero, Ahasver, appeared as the captain of a ship that seemed to sail the oceans forever. The ship did not look like the barge in which they had cruised only a year before. It was a three-masted warship replete with rusty cannons and worn rigging. At the end of the dream, Ahasver eventually made port and stepped onto the harbour where Josefina greeted him with an embrace. Ahasver responded to this tale by assuring her that he would be happy to embrace her without having to sail around the world in an ancient ship. The very next night, Josefina dreamt again. This time it appeared that Mark's castle estate was under a dreadful cloud that did not move for seven days but that on the seventh day the sunshine broke through to reveal a long-haired Jacky – or it could have been Yseult – dangling from the castle wall as she clung onto the outstretched hand of an unseen saviour. Ahasver smiled and said that this dream reminded him of the story of Joseph in Egypt that had been told to him when he was a boy in Holland. Josefina did not know that story but wondered what it might mean.

The arrangements for the wedding of Mark and Jacky were well advanced. The bride wanted the event to be notable in the annals of the region. Everyone who was anyone was invited – as well as local workers whom Jacky would not have recognised as anyone. The ceremony was to take place within the castle that had been sumptuously decked out for the occasion. The ball after the splendid meal was to feature a full orchestra playing for the guests and the dancers included many of Yseult's former ballet professionals. The one requirement for all the guests at the ball was to come in fancy dress. Josefina did not know that Ahasver intended to attend in the guise of a ghost. His mask bore a striking resemblance to Tristan. After the wedding ceremony itself, Mark seemed overwhelmed by the sheer volume of people thronging around the castle. He was so accustomed to it being a quiet, lonely place that the noise and lights, the music and the movement all made him feel quite giddy. Jacky, on the other hand, seemed almost intoxicated with this crowning achievement to all her plans. Her long hair now made her appearance so like that of her dead sister that Yseult's ballet colleagues quite forgot themselves and began dancing with her as if she were the celebrated ballerina. This simply made Jacky more excited as she was thrown around by lithe male dancers."

Sachs tried to speak with melodramatic emphasis: "The last dance is the Dance of death."

"It was nearing midnight when she found herself dancing furiously on the balcony of the ballroom. A partner with whom she had not yet completed a turn had her in his arms when he suddenly lifted her high above his head. She laughed as he carried her across the balcony to the clapping and cheering of the other dancers. An abrupt silence greeted his next move as he placed her over the edge of the balcony. He held her wrists and peered into her terrified eyes. She looked up and saw the face of Tristan glaring down at her. The voice from behind the mask announced that he had returned to hear his wife's confession. Until he had received it, he would leave her suspended. If she did not tell him why she had killed him within the next minute, he would let her drop to her death just as she had done to him.

It was within the hearing of over a hundred guests and Mark himself that Jacky's confession was spoken.

When she had finished, the ghost asked her why she had also killed her sister. Her blurted explanation was so confused that no one could understand exactly what she meant when she talked about her birthright, and her just reward in acquiring the husband she deserved. Ahasver finally lifted her back onto the balcony where one of the guests, the region's police chief, took her into custody. She looked imploringly into her husband's dumbfounded face as if seeking forgiveness; but could see no emotion there other than pity. Wrestling free from the policeman's grasp, she rushed to the edge of the balcony and threw herself over as the orchestra, unaware of the drama taking place on the balcony, played a pastiche of the final music of Wagner's music drama.

Mark King regained his castle as well as the wealth that had been illegally gained by his former wife (for Sir Tristan had no legal heirs). But he never regained a wife and died childless many years later. Josefina was released and became engaged to her flying Dutchman. Mark re-employed Ahasver to look after the estate. After the perennial wanderer married Josefina, he settled down promising his wife that he would never go on any more ill-fated barge trips. Josefina eventually took responsibility for running the affairs of the estate when Mark became too infirm to concentrate on the minutiae of finance and budgets. And it was to the married management couple to whom Mark bequeathed the estate in consideration of the wrongs that his wife had done them."

Sachs took a deep breath and walked back to his seat at the back of the room. No one clapped his performance and, to be brutally honest, I had not been convinced by his story. It felt long-winded – nearly twice as long as Sally's Odyssey! – and to me it felt contrived, as if he were paying respects to a long-lost tale and attempting, without success, to breathe new life back into it. I did not like it and, I suspect, I did not like Sachs. I don't know why I could not like him. Maybe it was because he sat, unmoving, week after week, at the back of the room as if not wanting to engage in the class. Perhaps I was envious that his story had been chosen to be read out loud whereas Sally's and my compositions had been ignored.

The Tzadik initiated a brief discussion about Sachs's story during which everyone (except me) politely praised this text, written by a man whose third language was English.

The Tzadik looked tired and said "I know that some of you like to address present day political issues directly in your writing. Others prefer to allude to them indirectly by reference to myths, fictions and humour. Left to your own devices now, what would you want to write? I shall be away for a little while. Whilst I am gone, Mr Sachs has offered to act as a post box. I would like you each to send one or two stories to him. Perhaps he can give marks before handing them back to you. Any that he feels should be taken forward for publication, he can forward to me. I shall meet you all again, hopefully, when I return."

BOOK TWO

BRAZILIAN TALES

I will admit to feeling quite hurt by how the Tzadik had treated us. After all, Sally and other young friends considered me to be an established author and composer. Yet he seemed to prefer the convoluted writing of a man like Sachs! Perhaps I had offended him in some way unintentionally. Or maybe, he always expected me to honour our shared Jewish heritage and felt I was wasting my time and energies in searching for meaning in other cultures.

I was determined to show him that he was wrong. I had long wanted to visit South America. One glance at the map immediately showed one giant country, larger than all of Europe put together, that contains a plethora of cultures. Brazil's past incorporated fascinating native societies, African slave traditions and waves of migration from various European countries – Portugal, France, Spain, Germany, England ... even Wales!

I decided to spend time in the most spectacular Brazilian city, Rio de Janeiro. Although I took several trips away from Rio up into Minas Gerais to Belo Horizonte, along the Costa Verde to Paraty, up north through Vitoria to Salvador and spending weeks in the inland towns of Petropolis and Ouro Prero, it was settled in a flat in Rio that I started to write these Brazilian short stories. Even whilst writing them, I imagined the Tzadik looking over my shoulder and shaking his head in disapproval at my vain attempts to escape his influence.

Whether I should bother sending them to Sachs, I would decide that when away.

FLORA

When Señora Da Flores gave birth to a daughter, she never guessed that the ugly child would make the family name into a world-famous brand. Baby Flora was born with a deformed spine. As she grew, the hunchback and ungainly appearance repelled other children from playing with her. So, Flora would play by herself up the hill. Her lawyer father, always unsure what gift to give so lonely a child, bought her first kite before she went to school. Her natural facility with kites showed itself early. Whilst other children and adults would gather to show off their elaborately decorated kites, Flora would stand some way off demonstrating brilliant aerobatics that others found hard to emulate.

Before finishing her unhappy time at school, Flora had already begun to develop the extraordinary two-handed technique with which she would win the world championship. Her control of the different kites that she had constructed was breath-taking. Her parents, whilst ashamed of not being able to alter their daughter's deformity which they felt was somehow their fault, were proud to watch her perform feats of kite flight. Her father noticed the competition challenge heralded in a national newspaper. The National Association in Brazil was looking for new talent to take on the best in the world who, apparently, flew their kites in China.

Despite the advertisement in the paper, very few came forward to show off their skills. Flora flew her kites watched by about twenty people and three judges. She was unknown beforehand and, despite winning the competition with ease, was still unknown. But she had secured her place in the upcoming world championship. The tournament took place in a cold European country: it was the first time that Flora had been outside the immediate confines of her region. Her father took her, and she carried her two kites carefully onto trains and planes – both forms of transportation being quite new to the young girl. When it came to her turn to perform, she was confused by the unfamiliar language, the unusual food, the plethora of officials, kite-makers, and competitive flyers. She later described the event as the worst disaster of her life. She took the two kites up, one in each hand, and when a gust flicked one against the other, both crashed to the ground in a pathetic heap. Señor Da Flores tried to console his daughter, but nothing could hide the fact that this was not to be her year.

Four years later, after Flora demonstrated once more why she should be a national representative, things were quite different. Accompanied by her father, she amazed the world of kite flying with a performance that had never been attempted. Using the skills she had been perfecting on the hill above her house, she took her two kites up and, after a few spectacular synchronised aerobatic displays that already could have won her the title, performed the trick that left her fellow competitors dumbstruck. She called it her "kite caress". The two kites moved together and then twisted their cords around one another in what she described as a "gentle embrace." The judges expected the kites to fall to the ground but, instead, she managed to take them up together in a spiral that untwisted the cords at their apex where they danced a celebratory victory roll before zooming down together and landing with grace at the judges' feet.

Dr. Li Ong, the Chinese champion, was the first to run across to Flora. He shook her hand and spoke at great speed to say that he had never experienced such virtuosity and that she deserved to be world champion no matter what the judges might think. Flora, who understood not a word of Chinese, was taken aback by such a show of affection and attention. She was so used to being shunned that Dr. Li made her feel like an embarrassed schoolgirl. She smiled her crooked smile and reached up her hand to shake Dr. Li's. To her surprise, Dr. Li took it without the customary grimace to which she had become accustomed whenever she approached another human being. He seemed quite unconcerned with her appearance: a man who clearly understood how she showed her character in flight rather than in her physique. Flora Da Flores felt that she had now reached the summit of her career. But this was merely the prelude to perhaps the most peculiar of love triangles.

Pippa Praia was born a couple of years after Flora. Her childhood could not have been more different. Her wealthy father and promiscuous mother separated before she went to school. Brought up by a maid employed by her absentee father, she and her older brother knew nothing of family life. The maid regarded the pair as troublesome and felt that her paid duties were little more than keeping them clean, fed and on time to school. Neither liked classes; the brother fell in with a gang who were a notorious nuisance in the neighbourhood whilst Pippa, being extremely pretty, received the unwanted attention of nearly all the gang members. Her brother's death, due to an overdose, affected her deeply. She knew he had developed a drug habit but thought he had got it under control by the time he had outgrown the teenage gang. Their father could not attend the funeral as he was off somewhere else in the world doing deals and making money. Their mother made one of her rare appearances accompanied by her latest partner, tossed a flower into the grave and departed after placing a perfunctory kiss on Pippa's cheek.

Feeling alone in the world, Pippa decided to improve herself by attending evening classes. Her decision was made as a direct result of seeing her mother. "Whatever happens to me," she said to herself, "I do not want to end up like her!" Her father agreed to pay her fees, and she started language lessons. But she found the intellectual challenge too much for her: lying sleepless at night trying to remember what the teacher had been imparting made her head spin. On her way to the class one evening, she heard laughter in the hall and peeped inside to see what was causing the commotion. The local amateur dramatic society was trying out a new play written by one of their members. It was a comedy and had clearly caught the mood of those present who were much amused by its quips and gags. Pippa stood at the back of the hall and was soon laughing along with the rest of the company. The elderly gentleman who acted as theatrical director to the happy band noticed Pippa and invited her to come and join them. "We need a pretty girl who can stand on the stage and catch the attention of the audience," he told her. That evening saw the end of Pippa's language lessons and the start of her career as an actress.

Acting careers do not usually follow a course like Pippa's. Although she enjoyed the fun of amateur dramatics, it was clear to the others that she had little talent for the stage. However, no one had the heart to inform her of her shortcomings. Instead, they let her invariably play the part of the dumb blond or mute Princess ... anything that did not require her to move about too much or speak. Blithely unaware of her weaknesses, Pippa believed she was the principal attraction of every show as her picture was always placed on the front of any advertising. Believing that she was now too big a star for the local theatre, she decided to try her hand at becoming a movie actress. She persuaded her father to rent an apartment near the television and film studios. Every day she walked to the studio and asked employees about how to make it in the business. She talked to them in the canteen, in the street outside, at the goods delivery door. She chatted to porters, cleaners, messengers, stagehands and even the odd actor. She got a job as the assistant to a lighting engineer with whom she had her first passionate affair. She left him when she was noticed by a producer who wanted an attractive girl to accompany him when negotiating deals to make it appear that he had some sort of sexual magnetism. One of his directors saw Pippa and took her off his hands, appointing her as a screen extra in one of the more unsuccessful soap operas being broadcast at the time. It was here that Pippa achieved her first leading role. The fact that she had nothing significant to say was not important as neither had any of the other characters.

Pippa was happier now than she had ever been. She had a job as an actress of sorts, lived in the city and, as a young attractive star of stage and screen, she enjoyed the attention of young men and women who frequented the bars and clubs around the studio. Her current partner, one of the soap's actors, was having a simultaneous affair with the secretary of the producer. Pippa had met the secretary, Sue Céu, and, although she did not like to admit it, found her more exciting than their shared boyfriend. It was at this moment that Sue, who enjoyed significantly more power than the producer would have liked to admit, made the momentous decision that was to change Pippa's (and Flora's) lives forever.

Sue Céu had been seconded to the television news team for a short period because of serious staff shortages. Flora had just won the world championship with her incredible kite display. The TV coverage showed the aerial performance as a special report – given extra coverage as the world champion was their national representative who, for the first time, had beaten the reigning world champion from China into second place. Flora was interviewed and her words were written down by Sue who decided, on her own, that Flora's appearance would not suit the brand of the TV channel. So, quite smitten by Pippa's glamour, Sue handed her the script and told her to read it out as part of an act. Pippa, totally unaware of the context in which she was being thrown, dutifully mouthed the speech that was filmed and broadcast as if she were Flora.

Flora's father was furious that his daughter was replaced on the screen "by some blond bimbo!" But Flora was already wiser than her parents when it came to the ways of the world. She had already seen and felt the way that people treated a woman with her disability and explained to her father how to behave. "When flying a kite, you must never fight the wind," she said. "You must recognise its power and use it to your advantage. It can be your friend, or it can destroy you: but it is always your decision as to how to face it. The first time I came to the championship, I thought I could beat the wind. Since then, I have learnt how to harness it. It is the same with people. Now I know how to use this to our advantage."

Dr. Li Ong was an inspiring aeronautical engineer. He oversaw a team of scientists developing new aircraft to serve the growing Chinese economy. A devoted party member from his teens, Li appreciated the discipline of clear structures and rules. His tutors at the University of Beijing awarded him the highest marks ever achieved from the normally over-strict Department of Physics. His great passion apart from his studies was flying the kites that he designed to reflect the latest ideas in aeronautical technology. When he won the Chinese kite-flying championship, he modestly put his success down to the quality of instruction given him by his university tutors.

As a model student and, later, a model manager, Li's success was due to his humility. He regarded himself as merely a hardworking extension of the scientists who had gone before him; some of whom he saw as having vastly superior talents to his own. So, when he was sent to represent his country in the world championship, he took a lively interest in other flyers' designs. Most followed well-researched models and he found that he could beat their performances with his well-worked routines. The only kites that attracted his attention were the strange structures built by Flora. When she flew them simultaneously, he was immediately impressed by the extraordinary skill she demonstrated by flying one in each hand with only her fingers acting as guides. Her odd hunchbacked appearance meant that she flew whilst naturally looking towards the ground. She seemed to sense their flight simply through her fingers. When they crashed together in the first championship, she was clearly crestfallen and ended up in tears beside her father. But Li could see that despite the disappointment, this was a real opponent who one day would be able to challenge him through sheer natural ability and individual design skills.

Four years later, Li – now overseeing the development of a new passenger aircraft at work – was again given leave to fly his kites for his country at the world championship. This time Flora's novel kites proved their manoeuvrability to be equal to his own meticulously crafted constructions. But the amazing skills she showed as a handler were unmatched. Li stood fascinated as she twisted the cords of the two kites without allowing them to lose height even for a second. Up and up they climbed, even though the inextricable complications of cords wound around cords meant that the physical rules of aeronautics must mean that they would end in a catastrophic dive. Whilst everyone else watched the phenomenal climb and the explosive unwinding victory rolls at the summit of the climb, Li glanced down at his opponent. She stood quite motionless, head bowed, and eyes closed. Her fingertip control of the kites was taking place with scarcely a movement. He wondered whether this apparent Zen master of the air had developed powers that were not yet understood by his fellow scientists. He looked up just as the kites unwound themselves and he knew that he was witnessing a new phase in kite flying from a woman who was many leagues ahead of himself and any other competitor present. He was so moved that as the kites landed, he rushed over to Flora to congratulate her. She seemed taken aback, but then he realised that an effusive outpouring of Mandarin Chinese probably meant little to the Portuguese-speaking woman.

Li returned home as runner-up to Flora Da Flores, determined to discover more of the secrets behind his victor's success. His curiosity was impelled partly by a desire to learn, although he knew in his heart that this would almost certainly make him into a mere emulator of the true virtuoso. But his main motivation was to explore any aeronautical innovations to be gleaned from this self-taught genius. He watched a recording of the televised final a few weeks later where he was seen applauding the winner's triumphant performance. But then he was totally bewildered when his opponent appeared as Pippa Praia.

To be the object of desire may be flattering. But, as Pippa was discovering, to be any kind of object frequently left you powerless – like some beautifully decorated plastic bag being blown about in the wind. When Sue Céu approached her a few weeks after her performance as Flora, she thought it might be to congratulate her and to offer her a new role. Instead, Sue informed her that the TV station had received a lawsuit from Señor Da Flores claiming damages against his daughter and threatening criminal proceedings on the charge of impersonation. The TV company was about to sack Sue, her producer and blacklist Pippa from ever having another part when they received a further offer from Da Flores which was one that the TV station was keen to accept. It offered to drop any charges against the company provided that two conditions were met. The first was that no one should be sacked, instead two named employees were to agree to carry out pre-set roles. First, Sue herself was to be given the job of overseeing an advertising campaign publicising Da Flores' kites on the TV station – a campaign to be carried without cost to the Da Flores' family. And the second condition was that Pippa was to agree to be the "new face of Da Flores' kites".

Pippa felt that the charismatic Sue had swept her off her feet with one sentence and landed her on a higher professional peak with the next. "You mean I am going to be a model? I may be famous?" Sue nodded. "Well of course we should accept, don't you think?" Sue nodded again.

The following weeks were a strange experience for Pippa. The future advertising campaign was to be dictated by her father, with his international business connections. Meanwhile, kites were being made on a small scale to Flora's design with Pippa's face and body displayed across their stretched material. Pippa was neither asked about, nor shown, the design nor the finished product. When Sue showed her one, however, she was delighted. "We ought to sell thousands of these," she told Sue; "then my face would be well-known all over the country." Sue told her that the Da Flores family did not have enough money to produce more than a pilot run. "No problem!" Pippa exclaimed. "I'll have a word with my father and get him to pay for lots to be made." And so it was that Pippa, without ever having met Flora Da Flores, nor knowing anything at all about kites, became identified as the face of kite flying.

Flora Da Flores had seen Pippa Praia in the flesh. As part of the deal, she asked her father to negotiate with the TV company. She was able to inspect the station's facilities, during which she could see how assertive Sue Céu was and how ineffectual her bosses seemed. Unseen by Pippa she watched as her impersonator appeared to worship Sue as she ordered people to do her bidding. But, more than anything else, she became aware of her own fascination with Pippa. If there was anyone whom she would wish to look like, it would be Pippa Praia. Everything that Flora lacked, Pippa seemed to possess. She carried herself with the carefree movement of a beautiful woman who enjoys others' attention. Flora sensed a strong bout of self-loathing – a sentiment from which she had suffered much as a child. But now it seemed to turn itself into a powerful attraction towards Pippa. It was during this visit that Flora devised the final offer that she instructed her father to make. Her father ensured that the unexpected investment from Mr.

Praia was in the form of a loan that was fully repaid from the profitable sale of kites. Pippa may well have regarded herself as the face of Flora Da Flores, but Señor Da Flores made sure that there was no way that she could claim any ownership of Flora's company.

Soon after the successful launch of her company, Flora received the invitation from Dr. Li to come to China. Li had moved heaven and earth to create a special aerodynamics research facility within the university dedicated to investigating innovations in his field. It was always his intention to focus its work on the seemingly impossible feats of kite flying achieved by Flora. He made it clear to his much-admired world champion that he would share any discoveries with her company. He also suggested that China would be the most profitable location in which to base any large-scale production of kites. Flora accepted and decided to decamp to Beijing. Separating Pippa from Sue was probably the only selfish act of her life. She told Sue that she wanted her to remain behind to handle the upcoming publicity campaign. Her father told Pippa that she was wanted for photo shoots in China where international publicity for mass produced kites required her image to be projected into the sky all over the world. But Flora also felt, quite irrationally, that without Sue present for Pippa to dote over, her alter ego might feel inclined to show some interest in the real Flora Da Flores.

On arrival in China, Pippa descended the steps of the aircraft and was greeted by hundreds of flag-waving admirers – each of them believing that they were seeing the real Flora Da Flores. She waved to them and immediately felt at home. Unnoticed by the crowd nor by

Pippa (who had still not met the great kite flyer herself), Flora made her way unsteadily down amongst the following passengers.

Pippa was swept off to an international hotel whilst Dr. Li greeted Flora and her father in a private room within the airport. Communicating through broken English, he explained that he would be honoured if they would stay with him in his house where they would be protected from the noise and bustle of the capital. "It is near a hill where I practise my own kite flying," he said; "and you would be able to go there every day if you wished."

The research about which Flora was the subject investigated the possibility of a computer programme connected to robot arms emulating the techniques that Flora had developed. Dr. Li left Flora to practise by herself as often as she wanted but asked her to demonstrate her skills in simultaneous flying to his team once a week. They registered every one of her movements and devised a programme that recorded everything she did. But when connected to the robot arms the difficulty in preventing collisions presented insuperable problems. The team worked on it until they felt that they had overcome the difficulties through well-analysed processes that had little to do with Flora's own performance. Meanwhile Pippa enjoyed the attention of photographers and newsmen anxious to capture her image and record her every move in night clubs, hotel restaurants and theatrical performances – in fact, everything that Beijing offered in terms of the high life. And still she showed no interest in meeting the real Flora Da Flores.

Flora read about Pippa's antics and wondered whether she could attract her attention. She decided that it was time that Dr Li spoke to Pippa and introduced her to the advertising team who were about to launch the first mass production of Flora Da Flores kites for international distribution. The pretext was to show her how her image was to bedeck the underside of every kite. The result of the meeting, however, was not as Flora had intended. Li regarded Pippa as a stupid waste of time; a mere dabbler in the serious business of aerodynamics and an impertinent impersonator of the genius currently residing at his home. But when Pippa met Li, she saw in him the man of her dreams. He was tall and handsome and, unlike her former partners, already a much-revered figure by everyone around him. He was obviously highly intelligent: he was both a father figure to a woman who had always lacked a real father and a desirable, unattached male to a woman who felt totally unattached in this exciting but strange land.

Flora observed how in the weeks that followed, Pippa made numerous attempts to get hold of Li – but none to contact her. Li, on the other hand, spent all his spare time discussing kites with Flora showing absolutely no interest in the messages sent by Pippa. She told her father that the peculiar triangle that had been created with her admitted fascination for Pippa, Li's constant pursuit of Flora's mysterious talent, and Pippa's frustrated attempts to arouse Li's interest, was the fragile basis upon which the company now rested. And so it continued with Pippa becoming older but no wiser; Li becoming wiser but not much nearer to understanding the roots of Flora's skill, and Flora quietly retiring to the hill in preparation for the next world championship. As the week of the championship approached, Flora's disability had become complicated by further deterioration of her spinal column. She was so unsteady on her feet that she often required the use of a wheelchair. Her father would push her up the hill with an assortment of her latest kite-creations. Li was sad to see his greatest inspirer become so disabled and wondered whether she might not be able to take part in the championship. But his fears were ungrounded.

The championship, held in China, featured Li himself as well as a special entry – his team's robot. Pippa sat proudly watching the performance as if she were the star of the show – and still she had never met Flora! She hoped that Li would win as he was her hero – she hardly gave a thought to the notion that Flora herself might be competing. But she did: and she produced a novelty whose meaning imparted itself powerfully to the astounded Li. First, she repeated her performance from the previous championship. Her simultaneous display had at last been successfully emulated by Li's robot. Then her double twisting demonstration ending in the unwinding flowering of the two kites at their apex again surpassed anything that her competitors could even attempt. But the new performance for which she had been practising showed artistry and craft beyond anything that Li nor his research team had even contemplated. Three strangely shaped kites drifted upwards. Li looked at Flora lying back on her wheelchair. She had a kite in each hand, and a third one with a string attached to each of her feet! He looked up and watched as the three seemed to circle one another. Her right-hand kite chased after the left, but the left ducked out of its way. Then the left seemed to chase the kite controlled by her feet. Again, the pursued kite ducked down and proceeded to chase after the right-hand kite. Again, and again the game of chase and avoidance was played out by the three players. Then the chase became more frantic. The lines started to twist together. Surely this was the inextricable confusion when they were bound to come crashing down. But it was now that the reason for the odd shape of the kites became apparent. As they meshed together, they miraculously clicked into the shape of a traditional kite, now controlled by six interlocking strings attached to all Flora's limbs. Wild applause broke out amongst the spectators. But still Flora had one more trick up her sleeve. With a flick of her wrists, she turned the aerially constructed kite over to reveal the words "Flora Da Flores" written across its underside. Pippa sprung to her feet to take the inevitable congratulations and was perplexed that the knowledgeable audience hardly noticed her as they sat, eyes upturned at Flora's winning performance, clapping furiously.

Four years later Flora could not compete. The deterioration in her spine left her with greatly diminished control over her limbs and she had retired to the mountains of Brazil from where her family had emerged. The Flora Da Flores company with its worldwide brand recognition kept her, her parents and her brothers and sisters in comfort for the rest of their lives. Balloons, blimps, kites – even rescue dinghies, yachts and a line of cosmetics carried the Da Flores name.

Pippa renamed herself Philippa Prior when she flew to Los Angeles to launch her career as a movie star after leaving Beijing. But the obvious difference between her youthful Flora Da Flores image and her appearance as an ageing amateur actress in the frequent auditions that she attended in a vain attempt to break into film left her as frustrated as she had been when pursuing Dr. Li. As she found that her Daddy's money was no longer forthcoming, she tried to claim money from the Da Flores company that she believed she had successfully represented. But Señor Da Flores had always worded contracts to preclude Pippa ever laying her hands on what he regarded as his daughter's earnings. So, after emulating her mother in so many ways, Pippa fell to emulating her brother. She spent as much time failing drug rehabilitation programmes as she had failed for all those years in seeking any meeting with Flora Da Flores.

Dr. Li also did not compete in the next world championship. One of his research team did ... and won after discarding all lessons learnt from the computer programmed robot. Li was by then fully involved in the development of the first mass produced passenger aircraft that was rolling off the production lines in central China. He had overseen its design, managed its production, and had been given permission (in consultation with the Da Flores company) to name the new fleet of aeroplanes Flora.

Sue Céu, now Manager of Da Flores Kites Brasil, was visiting the Da Flores home the day that Flora died. She was driving up the steep road when she saw a large asymmetrically constructed kite emerge above the ridge where Flora lived. She stopped the car to watch the kite.

It took her a few minutes before she realised that it was flying with no strings attached. Suddenly it was caught by the violent convection current caused by the harsh sun beating against the mountain's glinting rock face. The kite streaked upwards in a dramatic curve until it appeared as little more than a tiny dot in the blue sky directly above where Sue was standing. Shading her eyes, she saw it make a final summersault before disappearing over the summit of the mountain.

MONOLOGUE

"As you get older, you remember more." Sam was talking to his younger brother. At 98, Sam knew what he was talking about. He was 18 when his brother, Mark, was born so had always treated him as the baby of the family.

"When you get to my age, Mark, you'll recall all the details of our old house. I'll bet you don't remember the colour of the back door." Mark said nothing so Sam went on.

"It was blue. You see I even remember how many steps there were on the staircase up to our bedroom. There were fourteen!" Sam announced in triumph. He was quite proud of his ability to visualise the images of his childhood and recount the details of what he saw.

"The window at the top of the stairs always seemed dim. I suppose it was the weather outside. It was not like here where we have sunshine nearly all year. Grey skies and rain were normal, weren't they?" Sam reflected on the circumstances that had brought the two of them to this expensive residential home on the coast.

"Just because we had a dreadful climate did not mean we couldn't make lots of money. It was easy, wasn't it?" Even as a teenager, Mark had shown an entrepreneurial spirit and joined his brother in Sam's various ventures.

"You were a sharp operator, weren't you, Mark? I remember how you spotted that gap in the property market when everyone else was blind. You leapt in there with me, and we made a fortune! I'll bet they still curse us back home when we left them holding buildings and land that became almost worthless overnight. And what did we do? Huh! Talk about foresight! We bought this place and half a dozen like it all along the coast. That was even before we thought about getting old ourselves. We made even more money from the homes than we did with the little office blocks."

Sam fell silent and imagined angry people talking about "those brothers." He smiled as he remembered their trusty accountant, Maurice, telling them that he had lost track of how much money they had earned. "I don't know how many accounts you have in how many countries." And Mark had responded with, "Well if you don't know, then neither do the tax authorities," and they had all laughed.

"Did we ever pay tax?" Sam asked. "I'm sure that Maurice managed to arrange it, so we hardly paid anything. I'm afraid that I had to leave all that side up to you once my eyesight began to fail. And after Maurice died, we needed to simplify the business so at least we knew what was happening."

Sam thought back to the year when the auditor came to find out how much they owed the government: and

Maurice had died the day after the young man arrived. So, the books were inexplicable, and the auditor had to ask Mark what the various notes and figures meant. "Ah that means the income is taxed abroad," Mark had asserted again and again. "May I see the bank statements from the overseas banks?" the auditor had asked timidly. "Certainly not!" Mark had replied. "They are in the hands of auditors abroad so that they can assess how much we owe there."

"Why were you so nasty to that young guy?" Sam asked. "He was only doing his job. He became quite afraid of you. I would have been much more pleasant to him. I know you always said I was the smooth talker, getting the customers to part with their cash. You were the guard dog, protecting what we had from anyone who dared to imply that we owed them money. You were a soldier, and I was a civilian. Of course, you really went to war whilst I stayed at home – too old to serve the country. You must have been a fearsome warrior although I was always so worried about whether you would survive the battles where you won your medals.

Sam mused for a couple of minutes about bygone years. "Huh!" he exclaimed. "Do you remember when you told the bank that if they wanted our custom, they would need to reduce their charges. When the clerk refused, you withdrew a couple of million. The manager was on the phone to you within minutes negotiating special rates for us and begging you to keep our accounts with him." Sam laughed quietly. Then his thoughts turned to his late wife. "Was it all worth it?" was the question she had posed. "Did all that money make you happy?" she had asked just before the divorce. Sam never knew how to answer his wife. It had been Mark who provided her with the answer. "Money makes no one happy," he had said. "It just gives you more freedom of action."

"You were always the wise one," Sam said, nodding across the room to his brother. "You always had an answer to difficult questions. When the politicians approached us for contributions, I always admired the way that you extracted concessions from them even before parting with a cent. And the secret recordings you made of their conversations with you … my God! You could have had some of them in jail if you had wanted! But instead, you just used them to ensure that they delivered on their promises. That land concession you squeezed out of them must have made us into the richest partnership in South America!"

Sam started counting furiously on his fingers – an old habit that he had acquired as a child. Eventually, he completed his makeshift abacus-style calculation.

"No, you were right when you told me that we weren't the richest in the world. You said we were a bit behind one of the Arab sheikhs who had bought up lots of land in the capitals of Europe. But, with that exception, we must have been top – certainly in Brazil anyway."

Sam smiled as he basked in the glories of the successful business dealings of long ago. His breathing became shallower as he began to slip into a late morning snooze. A few minutes later he woke with a start.

"Sorry, Mark. I must have dozed off for a moment. I was dreaming of the time we went fishing in Alaska. I reckon that was the only time we competed where I won. That sock-eye salmon I caught was a real monster. I was dreaming of it hanging on my hook and wriggling whilst you shouted to the others to come and look at what I'd caught." Sam took a deep breath and stretched to wake himself up properly.

"Dreams like that make me hungry. Shall we go and have lunch now? Perhaps we can order salmon. Of course, you and your vegetarianism might mean I'll have to eat it whilst you just peck at the potatoes and peas." Sam laughed and was annoyed that Mark did not seem to share the joke.

"Come on, Mark. I was only joking. You know you can order anything you want. For myself, maybe I'll also have a glass of chilled beer to wash it down. I suppose you'll want fresh, filtered water or a fruit juice. I've always admired your discipline when it comes to food and drink. I've always just eaten anything I fancy and ignored the doctors who said I would never reach seventy. Most of them have long gone and here am I, still going strong, only a couple of years off a century!" The door opened and the young nurse walked in.

"Come on Sam," she said. "You shouldn't just sit in here all alone. Are those your brothers' service medals you're holding again? Why not put them back now so you can come and join us for lunch. We have nut roast which, as you know, is good for you."

REGRET

Virginia was walking in the rain when she was approached by a breathless, middle-aged man. He said "You have what I most desire. You have youth, you have beauty, and you have an umbrella. Would you care to share any of these with me?" Virginia told him brusquely to go and get his own.

A month later, Virginia was walking in the rain when the same man ran up to her. His appearance had altered remarkably. He was taller, sprightlier and more athletic. "Hello again," he said. "I did as you asked and have taken an elixir which has returned my youthful looks. However, I still can't find a decent umbrella. Would you care to share yours with me?"

Taken aback, Virginia refused. So, the man ran off into the rain. As the distance between them lengthened, he seemed to get slower and older with every pace. Eventually he disappeared and has never been seen again. There are times when Virginia regrets withholding the shelter of her umbrella. But she consoles herself with the thought that she has never got wet.

SCOOP

Dear Son

I watched your moving speech last month at the funeral of our greatest artist, Max Pintor. As our President, you put into words what many people feel. Pintor seemed to encapsulate and represent much of our nation's history and culture and what it stands for. His most famous picture, the so-called 'Lisard', attracts hundreds every day to the National Gallery. Your challenge that we should try to discover the identity of the Lisard naturally caught my attention as a journalist.

The panoramic view of Pintor's masterpiece shows scores of characters who demonstrate the racial and cultural diversity of our nation. Many are clearly realistic portraits; some are shown only in shadowy outline. But at the centre is the curiously elongated figure that has given the painting its nickname. Most commentators have described the Lisard as a metaphorical symbol of the heart of our country – not as a portrayal of a real person. However, I decided to travel back to the coastland to investigate myself. After all, I may have the advantage over earlier investigators in that I know the area well and speak the local dialect.

I discovered that the Lisard was real. He was born into a family of eight children, one mother but several fathers. He never knew his father, but the man was clearly of a far darker hue than the others as the Lisard was much blacker than any of his brothers and sisters. He was also much taller and walked with a characteristic stoop as he was self-conscious about his height. At school, he found the lessons easy but deliberately provided incorrect answers in tests so that he would not be teased about being clever.

As a teenager, he hung around the beach with his three friends. They were well-built, noisy, shiny, and black or brown. He was slender, quiet and a matt blue-black in colour. They would swim together; and the Lisard always made sure that he did not swim too fast to outstrip his friends in their races. It was whilst they lounged on the beach that Pintor saw them as he frequented the local bar which overlooked the beach. I spoke with the current bar owner who bought the bar from the previous owner. The previous owner was a small man who knew Pintor well as a regular customer, and often boasted of it. He claimed that Pintor painted his masterpiece whilst renting a room upstairs: but this seems unlikely as above the bar there is only a tiny room with no light. He also employed the Lisard briefly to collect glasses and serve customers but dispensed with his services when he found attractive female customers paying more attention to his waiter than to him.

The Lisard, having left school and having lost his job, would take out his frustrations at the end of the afternoon by swimming alone across the bay. He swam with an intensity that attracted the attention of the local coastguard. This friendly older man suggested that he could come become a lifeguard. The Lisard followed his advice and qualified quickly. Then he disappeared from the immediate area as he was allocated a beach some distance away. He rented a small flat near his workstation and patrolled his patch attentively. In the evenings he began to keep a detailed diary of what he felt and saw – but he would never let any passing partner read it.

It was a year later that he saw the girl fall from the back of a passing boat. Her companions, city folk out for a sunshine weekend, were too drunk to notice her demise and the boat continued up the coast leaving her flailing about in an area with dangerous currents. The Lisard dashed out and swam to her rescue. He brought her onto the beach where she got over her shock quickly. However, she never got over her rescuer and returned many times to be with him. When they got married, her father, the editor of a newspaper in the capital, demanded to know why she would want to marry "a beach bum". But she saw more in her husband than that.

It was after reading his diary that she suggested that his writing skills were far too good to remain hidden. He said he was quite happy as a lifeguard. She said she knew only too well how good he was at his work, but still felt he should give writing a chance. So, under marital pressure, he went to college and was rewarded by being given a job as a junior reporter by his father-in-law. By this time, he needed more income as their son had been born. So, he worked hard and became a senior reporter before their son started school.

I think you have probably guessed by now that you are the son of the Lisard. My instinct as a journalist is to publish this scoop before anyone else realises who I am. However, in view of next year's Presidential election, I thought you might like to release the information at the best moment. After all, it cannot harm your prospect of re-election to be known as the son of the most potent symbol of our nation!

Love
Dad

THE CLICHÉS OF LIFE
(a story for the Tzadik)

He was bold as a lion, her knight in shining armour. Yet he was gentle as a lamb, butter would not melt in his mouth. But Fanny, a blond bombshell and her best friend, had warned that he was a wolf in sheep's clothing and advised her to give him a wide berth. And the proof of the pudding was in the eating. Instead of sticking by her through thick and thin, he had gone off the rails and forsaken her for another woman. She did not know who her rival was: but she was a snake in the grass, a Jezebel ready to snare her man the moment her guard was down. And he had fallen for her hook line and sinker.

She had always believed that slow but steady wins the race. But in the race of life, fortune favours the brave and to the victor the spoils. Bold as brass, she had confronted him: "Don't you understand that united we stand, divided we fall? Are you a man or are you a mouse?" He answered with a squeak. Now she felt like death warmed up. That morning, she had got out of bed the wrong side. Sitting alone with her diary, she had counted the days since they had met. Six hundred!

Perhaps it was time to end it all. She decided to walk to the nearby cliff and throw herself off. After all, life was not worth living without him. He was a pillar of the community, the best thing since sliced bread, the man with the Midas touch. She reached the edge of the world and looked down, a bottomless pit. She thought of every day she had known him and said to herself "into the valley of death rode the six hundred" but could not quite remember where she had read those words.

Fanny had tried to put heart back into her. A friend in need is a friend indeed. Fanny told her that having learnt her lesson the hard way, she would feel that once bitten twice shy. However, it was important to keep her pecker up and never say die. After all, there are plenty more fish in the sea. She said, "it's better to have loved and lost, than to have never loved at all." But if knowledge is power, she did not feel any of the life force within her. She was out of tune with the times, an old-fashioned girl with a black and white sense of right and wrong. Not like Fanny who always seemed dressed to kill. She had even seen her friend enter his house. "Did you persuade him to change his mind?" she asked. Fanny replied that she had pressed him in every way she knew how. But he seemed bent on sowing his oats elsewhere.

What effect would her final act, her curtain call, have on the unseen she-devil and that chicken-livered apple of her eye? She knew that two is company and three is a crowd; but had never thought she would be the odd one out. "Too many cooks spoil the broth" her mother used to say ... and her broth had certainly been spoilt. She wondered how many others had taken the plunge over Lover's Leap. She imagined as they flew down the cliff face, they would think that birds of a-feather flock together before they hit the ground.

She had a vision of how she would appear in the newspapers the next day. Perhaps she would be portrayed as a sleeping beauty to tug the heartstrings of all those she would leave behind. Suddenly it was as if she caught a glimpse of a photograph: it was of her flattened body – a fish out of water. This would be a fate worse than death. It would offend her well-developed sense of style and language, so she turned back to continue life's journey.

One evening, remembering the Tzadik's appeal that I should know more of the famous English writers of the eighteenth century, I was reading Alexander Pope's poem 'Eloisa to Abelard' and came across the phrase 'Eternal sunshine of the spotless mind!' I had no idea that this is where the classic film directed by Michel

Gondry had got its name. That night I dreamt a story that may have been inspired by Pope's description of someone blameless.

> *How happy is the blameless vestal's lot!*
> *The world forgetting, by the world forgot.*
> *Eternal sunshine of the spotless mind!*
> *Each pray'r accepted, and each wish resign'd;*
> *Labour and rest, that equal periods keep;*
> *Obedient slumbers that can wake and weep*

from Eloisa to Abelard   by Alexander Pope

THE CLOUDMAKER

No one knows from where he came. He appeared in our town one Spring and most believed him to be a travelling salesman. Dressed in a slightly crumpled suit, he walked with the stoop of a man uncomfortable with his above-average height. After a week in the Hotel Parana during which time he sold nothing to anyone, he walked into the new estate agency in the Town Square and asked to view an empty property that was perched above the town on Crooked Mountain. Nobody had lived there for many years, but he seemed satisfied with the outlook and bought it for cash. Gossip turned to guessing who he was. He was clearly no salesman.

Farming in the surrounding countryside was increasingly difficult as rain became less frequent.

Occasional drought conditions had already led to the failure of one or two smallholdings. The stranger, now established overlooking the farmlands as far as the eye could see, began talking to arable farmers about how much water they would need to fall on crops each month. Still believing him to be some sort of salesman, farm owners asked if he had water supplies to sell. He told them he could provide them with water for free but needed to know the quantities required. Opinion now turned to regarding him as an eccentric, but harmless, idiot with notions of grandeur that made him appear ridiculous to the sensible folk who lived down on the plain. Nonetheless, he was given the information he requested as no one felt that it would matter what he knew.

The rainy season began, as usual that year, with no rain. But a week later, unpredicted by the weather forecast, large cumulus clouds came billowing over the ridge of Crooked Mountain. They deposited large quantities of rain on the grateful farmers' fields. By the end of the season, it was noted that exactly the amount of rain required for a successful crop had fallen. The cloudmaker on the mountain had scored his first success although, at the time, no one believed that he had anything to do with the weather. But when he appeared at local farmers' meetings asking whether the same quantity would be welcome the following year, he was told that it would be greatly appreciated if he would not waste their time with ridiculous claims.

The following year he invited the local school to bring classes up to his property so that they could learn geography by having the teacher point out rivers, roads and landmarks from his vantage point. Some enterprising teachers took him up on the offer. It was during one of these school trips that a class group watched with amazement as the man seemed to create clouds of different shapes and sizes and launch them across the sky with a flourish that led to happy applause from the youthful audience. The teacher, puzzled but curious, challenged the cloudmaker to repeat his performance. Instantly clouds were made with a running commentary from their maker. "These are functional, full of water, and easily shaped to look like familiar objects," he said as cumulus clouds danced across the ridge. The children laughed as they recognised the shape of a goat, and another with the shape of a horse whose shadow seemed to gallop across the fields. "Of course, there are times when I feel stressed or angry and this shows as towers of thunder crash across the land," he said as a giant nimbus cloud appeared. The children fell silent, and a chill wind flashed briefly down the slopes and into the town. "But my favourite is the delicate traceries I can carve high up in the sky," he smiled as flecks of cirrus scurried above them and the sun reappeared.

News soon spread of the cloudmaker's accomplishments. Farmers who had previously regarded the man as a lunatic came banging on his door with gifts and requests to bring rain to their fields again. The cloudmaker obliged but was continuously heard to insist that his powers were not infinite and that he could not always produce what they wanted on demand. One day he would not be able to give them what they wanted. Some townsfolk said that as rain was not guaranteed, they were thankful because they preferred dry to wet weather. But for the second season in a row, the farmlands produced bumper crops as the correct quantity of rain was delivered at exactly the right moment.

Rico Gobo, the owner of the local newspaper, published an article about the cloudmaker. Initially these were amongst stories about people whom he regarded as amusing characters: the cloudmaker was painted as a fantasist who lived an eremitic existence up a mountain. After the school children incident, Gobo took the position of regarding the cloudmaker as a competitor for his position as undisputed principal power in the region. Mentions of the cloudmaker in the paper were dry and unfriendly. They implied that his motives for bringing the children to his house were devious. They cast doubt upon whether rain falling on the fields had anything to do with the man on the mountain. One edition ran an entire pullout section about the natural circulation of water; oceans heated by the sun forming clouds blown over land, falling as rain that flowed back to the sea down rivers – the first and last education supplement of Gobo's newspaper.

None of this seemed to affect the cloudmaker. He was heard to worry about his declining skills. He was worried that his age had started to affect the intensity of his cirrus creations. Yet his creativity did not appear to have waned as people watched the products of his work sail overhead. And his service to the local farmers continued unabated. One year, whilst he was demonstrating his abilities to a university team whose research was funded by Gobo, he spoke about other cloudmakers whom he had not seen for many years. He said he missed their company but that cloudmaking was, by its very nature, an individual activity. The research concluded that there was evidence to suggest that the cloudmaker was part of an organised network with potential conspiratorial intent to subvert the natural course of nature. The cloudmaker was visited by officials from the Ministry of Defence with an eye to using his talent as a weapon. Drowning the enemy in torrential rain could become a useful addition to the army's arsenal. But the cloudmaker seemed unwilling to rent his skills for military purposes: and Gobo ran an article explaining how citizens were either supporters of society or they were its enemies. Refusal to support the government's reasonable requests to help "our boys who are fighting for our country" was tantamount to treason.

The lightning strike upon Gobo's newspaper building was headline news even in national papers not owned by the magnate. No one was hurt but suspicion fell upon the cloudmaker. Perhaps he was angry at what Gobo had published in the previous weeks. Perhaps he even intended harm to come to Gobo himself. Gobo commissioned a company to build him a lightning-proof vehicle in which he felt he might travel in safety. The company provided him with a car with rubber tyres ... and charged him a fortune for their time! This was when I arrived on the scene as a young reporter employed by Gobo. My reputation was based purely on articles that I had written for the university news sheet – a ridiculously hyped-up reputation as a fearless reporter who had blown the cover on how some academics made more money on the side by exploiting what they had learnt or discovered whilst employed at public expense. Now I was being asked to blow the cover on the cloudmaker. Instead of focussing on his façade of goodness, I was asked to reveal his ambitions and discover how he felt about my wonderful employer, Rico Gobo.

My first expedition up the mountain was totally fruitless. The cloudmaker was not at home. The house seemed deserted. I reported back and the editor (Rico Gobo's son) asserted that this was evidence of the cloudmaker running away after attempting to murder his father. My second visit, a week later, found the cloudmaker in his garden looking quite serene. I introduced myself and launched straight into a description of the fear induced by the lightning strike. The cloudmaker shook his head and hoped that no one had been hurt. He explained that he had been absent all that week and that the weather was not his responsibility when he was not there. I asked for evidence about where he had been, and he smiled. "I do have other cloudmaking friends," he said. "I do miss them and felt I deserved a small holiday." Then he asked me what cloud formations had been like whilst he had been away. I recalled that the sky had been covered most of the time with an unusual slate grey sheet that stretched to the horizon. "Huh! Stratus formations!" he exclaimed. "I never make stratus clouds: far too boring. They must have blown over from the sea." I asked him where he had been so that I could check out his story of absence: but he made it clear that the person whom he had visited would not welcome any intrusion into her private life.

I wrote an article describing the cloudmaker's claim of absence and providing the presence of stratus clouds as his only alibi. The editor then appended a further paragraph implying that the cloudmaker's absence was for sexual gratification and that there was no reason to believe that he could not have launched the lightning attack from a distance. Then he sent me back up the mountain to see what effect the article had had upon its victim. To my surprise, I discovered that the cloudmaker was completely unaffected by anything that was written as he did not read our newspaper. I showed him the article and he frowned. "Did you write this?" he asked. "Most of it," I replied. "Then you should be ashamed of yourself." He looked me in the eye, and I knew that he was offended not through guilt but through righteous indignation. "Perhaps it would be better for my own peace of mind not to read anything from your paper in future," he said as he went back into his house.

More from pique than anything else, I posted a copy of the following week's edition in which my boss wrote an editorial directly addressed to the cloudmaker. In it he challenged the man he regarded as his family adversary to prove his mastery over the weather. "If you can control the clouds as you claim, then you should be able to prevent catastrophes like the one you visited upon us. You could give us sunshine! So, we shall regard all clouds that come over us in future as ones that you have sent, uncalled for." The gauntlet had been thrown down by the Gobos and it was down to the cloudmaker to respond. Weeks passed and nothing happened. No message was received from the man on the mountain. The Gobos laughed. The damage caused by the lightning strike was minimal, but they had exaggerated its effect in the report carried by the paper: I know because the broken window and slightly charred desk were in my office. The paper carried another article commenting upon the lack of response from the cloudmaker.

Two weeks later, strangers were seen climbing the road towards the cloudmaker's house. They were a motley crowd, some old and some youthful: some formally dressed and others looking more like hippies with long hair and strange clothes. Smelling a story, I decided to follow them. When I knocked at the door, the cloudmaker opened it. "Oh, it's you," he said with evident disappointment. "You had better come in but don't cause a fuss." I walked in and found about twenty people holding drinks and chatting in a variety of languages. The cloudmaker beckoned me across to a young woman with long, black hair and extraordinarily dark brown eyes – the irises were almost black. "This is the woman I was visiting when your office block was struck by a freak bolt of lightning. She is my daughter." I shook her hand. She nodded politely and walked away. "Now go and sit over there and keep quiet," he commanded. Then he clapped his hands, and the party fell silent as he spoke to them for about ten minutes. They asked a few questions which he answered amid some laughter. But the content of the speech was incomprehensible as they spoke in a tongue I did not recognise. When the talking was over, the people broke up into groups and the cloudmaker came over to me. "You can tell your boss that we have agreed to prevent any further clouds reaching this region. All cloudmaking here is to be down to me." "Who are these people?" I asked. "They are my fellow artists and have agreed to the request unkindly phrased by your editor. Now you may go."

I raced back to the office to write up my scoop. The editor was delighted. His editorial commentary spoke of the "cabal of cloudmakers convened by the arch-wizard who lives in our midst." He went on to ask for all citizens to report any untoward meteorological events so that the cloudmaker could be held to account. But the weather behaved itself perfectly that year with exactly the required rainfall requested by the local farmers. Otherwise, the days were bright and the nights pleasantly cool. By the end of the year, it was clear that little was to be gained by simply recording the weather: so, I ventured up the mountain again to see if I could discover more about our reclusive artist. I found him in his garden pruning his flowers. He let me stand beside him as he continued his work. He seemed unusually chatty – perhaps missing company he was happy to talk to his otherwise unwelcome visitor. Without thinking, I asked about his daughter and whether she ever came to see him. He wiped his forehead and told me that since his wife died, he had not seen as much of his daughter as he would have liked as she spent most of her time with her own work – and her children. This was an entirely different dimension to the cloudmaker that I found difficult to absorb. He was a grandfather! I looked at him and saw a man who suddenly seemed older than the one painted in our articles. I decided to tell nobody about this unplanned and unannounced visit. For the first time, my journalist's instinct told me to remain silent.

Without further reports concerning the cloudmaker, my editor reassigned me to cover stories further afield. For three years, I covered events abroad. A couple of times I thought that I had glimpsed people who had been at the cloudmaker's house, but I could never be certain. Therefore, it was with some surprise that I received a note from his daughter. It said that her father had developed his skills to such an extent that he wanted to give a demonstration. He wondered whether I would care to return home to watch the show. It gave a date and time – nothing more. I contacted my editor who suspected that I had cooked up the story just to obtain a holiday at home for free. Rather than have a dispute with my employer, I agreed to take a holiday and pay for the return home myself. On arrival I immediately climbed the hill to call on the cloudmaker. I was disappointed not to find him there. Peering up to the top of the mountain, however, I saw a slow-moving figure amongst the rocks. Clambering carefully up the gravel and treacherously loose stones, I eventually reached him. It was the cloudmaker looking much older now and out of breath. I spoke first: "Why are you up here?" "I am trying to gauge the optimum position for the demonstration tomorrow," he said. "What are you going to do?" I asked. "I shall show you what you can enjoy when I am gone," he answered enigmatically. "Come up here tomorrow and I shall show you everything."

The next day saw several of his friends gathered in the town. But none seemed to want to climb the hill. I set off by myself. The cloudmaker had perched himself on the rocks overlooking his house and waved to me happily. The sun was shining, and he seemed to be enjoying himself. "Only a few minutes to go now," he shouted. "Watch the sky." I looked up and saw nothing of interest. The sky was blue and only a few patches of cloud flecked above us. A few minutes passed and the clouds seemed to be closing together into a few light patches. "I am ready!" the cloudmaker shouted. I looked at the clouds again and was astonished to see what he had achieved. Each patch had been shaped into a circle and the surface facing downwards had been stroked into a fine sheen – a reflecting mirror. Later, some of his friends told me that they had counted fifty of these amazing mirrors that flashed their reflected light onto the land below. The cloudmaker had given us a string of suns that stretched to the horizon!

The cloudmaker made his way gingerly down the slope as his suns slowly dissipated. When he reached me, he asked "Did you enjoy that little spectacle?" I said that I was amazed at what he had done but puzzled by the message I had received from his daughter. Why had he not invited me himself? "She sometimes helps me when I am developing something new," he replied. "But she is more naturally gifted than me so really I ought to act as her secretary," he smiled. "She thought you ought to view your future before I took my leave." I frowned and asked if he was going away for a long time. He turned and shook my hand. Surprised by his move, my quizzical look must have amused him. He laughed and said, "Goodbye now." Then he walked into his house, leaving me to wonder how I was to report this strange encounter.

I decided that, as I was officially on holiday, I did not need to file a report. Again, and only for the second time, my journalist instinct told me to write nothing yet. I sauntered down to my parent's old house where I knew I could take refuge whilst pondering how to proceed. A week passed and I met some old friends; but did not go near the newspaper office. Another week passed and I knew that as my vacation was ending, I would need to decide how to account for what I had seen and heard. The paper had not even mentioned the astonishing solar reflection display: it was as if it had never happened. Now I was beginning to doubt the memory of my own eyes. Was I sure of what I had seen? I asked friends and most said they had noticed nothing untoward. But a few confirmed that they had seen the remarkable sight; but some of those wondered whether it had been a trick of light or their imagination. It was on the last day of my break that I received the final communication from his daughter. All it said was: "Are you interested in buying my father's house?"

Confused, I walked along to the estate agent. How did the daughter know that I was wanting to buy a house of my own rather than stay at my parent's place whenever I was in town? Why did she think that her father would want to sell his mountainside retreat? I asked the estate agent about the house. "Ah yes; the cloudmaker's place," he winced – a twisted smile that told of hundreds of property sales to customers whose money he felt should be his own. "You can go and inspect it at any time as the owner is no longer there." "I don't need to see it," I replied, "I want to know why it is on the market." "Hmm," the agent demurred as if the truth might damage the prospect of a sale. However, he decided that he might as well get the hard part over before speaking of the wonderful views, the vacant possession and the competitive price. "The owner died last week."

I have lived in the cloudmaker's house now for ten years. I have never seen his daughter again nor any of the cloudmaker's friends and colleagues. Yet his presence seems to permeate the place despite many attempts to impose my own personality on the house. There are occasions when I peer into the clear blue sky in the hope of seeing yet again one of his creations: but the blank canvas is all that ever meets my gaze. We have had no rain whatsoever for a decade. It is what we asked for and it is what we got. The solar display was not only a work of art, but it was also a prophecy and warning. Perhaps the only escape from the drought brought upon us would be if I could find the cloudmaker's daughter and ask her to reverse her father's legacy. But it as if she were herself made of ethereal cloud as no trace of her or her children's existence can now be found. My final article for the Gobo newspaper was entitled 'The prospect of eternal sunshine'.

BOOK THREE

TALES FROM NOWHERE

Inspiration for a writer can come from travelling to new places and seeing new people. I do not believe, like the Tzadik, that the exploration by the artists into the heartlands of one's own culture and upbringing should be more than enough for any artist. So, with a metaphorical thumbing of my nose to our teacher, I decided to set off and leave Brazil. In the following few years, I visited many lands – but never stayed in any one place for long. My stories during that period are 'Stories from Nowhere' in particular. Throughout those years I asked myself is attachment to any piece of land essential (as specified by those Zionist students who had challenged the Tzadik) or is the Tzadik right in asserting that that is just another delusion? Can we create stories without any attachment to the land in which we happen to be living? Does a writer need a home?

TO SEE THE SEA

Sue had never seen the sea. As she lay in bed that morning, her thoughts turned as usual to her dream of visiting the seashore and letting the waves splash her feet. Then she imagined she would warily step forward and allow the delicious feeling of water playing around her legs increase as she walked further into the sea. She closed her eyes and saw herself swimming lazily through the foamy water as the sun warmed her back.

Of course, she had seen the sea on television. She must have watched more programmes about beach holidays than anyone on the estate where she lived. But there had always been a good reason why she was unable to travel to the coast. When she was young, her parents never ventured far from the town and had little or no money to spend on holidays. When she married Ed, he had promised that they would go to a faraway resort once they had saved enough. But the birth of their son had eaten up most of Ed's paltry income, and when their daughter was born two years later, they had barely enough to pay for what they had borrowed to buy their little house.

Ed worked hard but the company was going through hard times so none of the employees were given pay rises – apart from the directors whom Ed called 'the Jaguars' as this was their car of choice as they swept out of the gates each evening. So, when their son left school and managed to get a job in the capital, they were pleased that he would better himself although sorry that they would only see him rarely. And when their daughter married a lad she had met at college, they were happy that he seemed a nice boy from a hill farm although they were only too aware that his parents believed he had married beneath him.

They had saved to pay for their daughter's wedding – although clearly not enough to convince her in-laws that she and Ed cared about the marriage. But once the young couple went to live out in the country, Sue was determined to save so that she could, at last, take their long-delayed trip to the coast. Then Ed got ill. She was sure that it was work-related and said that she could smell nasty odours whenever she passed the factory. Ed's insistence that this was not the case as he worked some miles from the factory in an office attached to the warehouse complex did nothing to persuade Sue that she was wrong. When the Jaguars forced him to retire on grounds of ill health, the money he brought into the house dropped and the ever-receding goal of a coastal holiday looked further off than ever.

A disabled woman who lived up the hill advertised for a cleaner and Sue was the first to apply. Mrs Box had her funny ways. She liked to sit at the window and eat her sandwiches off a plate on her lap. She liked to watch television via a reflection in a mirror as she insisted that all TVs gave out harmful rays so should not be viewed directly. But she always paid Sue cash at the end of the week – even though the amount never altered and hardly compensated for the fall in Ed's income. Nonetheless, Sue managed to save a tiny sum every week and put it towards fulfilling her dream.

When Ed's condition worsened, the doctor recommended that he leave the town and breathe some fresh air. Sue asked if that meant they ought to go and spend some time by the sea, but the doctor shook his head. "Mountain air is best," he pronounced. So, her small savings, together with money their son sent them, were spent on taking Ed to a little guesthouse in the hills. She did not enjoy their time up there. It was far away from her friends and neighbours and the local people seemed unfriendly. Ed's condition improved but when they got back home, he became ill again. He found it hard to breathe and coughed all day and night. When he died, the family came together for the funeral and then disappeared back to their own lives.

As she lay in bed, Sue could hear the traffic outside. She had become accustomed to the noise for many years but recently had become aware of its intrusive nature. Worse still was the occasional roar of the aircraft as they took off from the nearby airport reminding her of those lucky enough to be flying off to sunny beaches abroad. Mrs Box would be waiting for her; so, she got up, washed and dressed quickly in clothes that she had always worn when visiting Mrs Box, and gulped down a coffee in place of breakfast. She knew that Mrs Box could easily afford to pay her more, but she had never had the temerity to request a pay rise. Now that the house had been paid for from Ed's company's life insurance scheme, she felt that every coin she earned should be put towards the journey to the seaside. The desire for this trip was now so great that she thought it would overcome her natural inhibitions when confronting Mrs Box.

When she arrived at the house, however, Mrs Box was not there. Instead, her son whom she had never met opened the door with the news that his mother had decided to go on holiday and would not be back for a month. Sue was taken aback as she had never known her employer even to want to leave the house. Taking her courage in both hands, she said something that was not strictly true. She asserted that his mother had promised to pay her regularly every week whether she was at home or not. So, she would continue to clean the house and would expect to be paid as usual. The son shrugged his shoulders and said he knew nothing of this arrangement but was happy to pay her whatever was owed. He asked what the sum would be and Sue, telling a deliberate lie for the first time in her life, cited a sum that was significantly more than Mrs Box had ever paid. The son took out his wallet and paid her a full month in advance because he said he did not expect to be at the house very much.

When Sue returned home, she laid out the money. It was more than she had ever held at one time. She knew that she could now afford to buy a ticket to the seaside and stay in a little hotel that had advertised a special cheap rate in the local paper the week before. She carefully packed her best clothes in an old suitcase that Ed's parents had given them as a wedding present. When she went to bed, she was excited to think that the next day she would wake up, walk to the station, and leave the town for a whole week.

The train journey seemed to take forever: but Sue enjoyed every minute. She watched as the fields paraded their way past the carriage window displaying moody cows grazing and happy horses trotting about their green domain. She could see the sun glinting on the roofs of the splendid houses that bestrode the passing hillsides. She experienced a delicious sense of growing excitement as the train began to nuzzle into the resort, and colourfully dressed people walked before rickety houses and shops. As the train drew into the station, she saw the platform as if it were a carpeted strip onto which she had promised herself a grand entrance. She glided her way out of the station and into a waiting taxi. The driver knew the hotel and whisked her there in no time at all. The receptionist was so polite and helpful that Sue felt she had become royalty overnight. Dropping her little case in her neat and tidy room, she decided to walk immediately to the seashore. The walk took ages because the hotel was not near the front; but Sue did not mind. She was able to peer into the boutiques selling sun cream, postcards and various, beach attire. She liked it that she could take her time, as the sea would be there when she arrived at the beach. The expectation of delight was to be savoured as much as the actual final dipping of her feet into the water. None of the boutique fare attracted her for she knew that all she wanted was to feel the salty water lapping on her bare skin. At last, she saw the horizon with nothing but sea as far as she could see. The sand looked inviting as she made her way down the steps onto the beach. The sun had made it hot, but she cared not a jot as she kicked off her shoes and walked determinedly towards the water. The sound of the sand and shingle being continuously turned over merged with the unfamiliar screech of huge sea birds dipping and weaving overhead. Sue smiled as, at last, her dream became a reality, and she entered the waves. She caught her breath as the coldness of the water touched her legs; but she closed her eyes and tried to prolong the moment for as long as possible. This was the ocean that had been calling her for so many years; and now she was accepting its invitation.

    Concerned that his mother was not at home all weekend, Sue's son decided to call in as he was passing on business the next day. He knew that his mother never left the house for very long and was worried that something had happened to her. He felt that she had not really recovered from the shock of his father's death: she seemed in a world of her own whenever they had spoken afterwards. He let himself in with the key that had once been on his dad's key ring. He called out, but there was no answer. It took him a few minutes before he discovered her under her threadbare blankets, lifeless, with a small pile of money beside her bed.

THE COMPENDIUM OF PAIN

Reviewing a book by an author one knows personally is never easy. Evelyn, as I knew him, was a difficult man with whom to communicate. He was frequently silent and introverted. His previous life as a woman was something about which he never spoke. I suspect that his sex change operation was fundamentally a failure as it did not bring him any of the results that he dearly sought.

His book, 'The Compendium of Pain', has many of the features of the obsessive listings of sexual activity in '120 Days of Sodom' although unlike De Sade, Evelyn seems only interested in the internal sensation of pain – not its infliction. It details pains from the slightest discomfort to the most excruciating agony. It goes into the varieties of pain that can be felt by every nook and cranny of the body. He describes the natural pains of childbirth (a rare insight into his former life as a woman) and what he calls the "unnatural" pain caused by the surgeon's knife. His prolonged diatribe in which he addresses acute pain contrasts sharply with the section in which he explains how chronic pain can be moderated by a series of yoga exercises. Much of the book is extraordinarily tedious: this is not a book written to be read.

Whilst ploughing through the 'Compendium', however, one is struck by the lengths to which Evelyn goes to describe pain. The lack of language available to capture the vast variety of aches and pains is compensated by his acquisition of visual and auditory imagery in pursuit of a satisfactory vocabulary. Tactile formulations are used to a fuller extent than I have read in any book: but the sheer immensity of the task he set himself, to list in an encyclopaedic fashion the full extent of pain's empire, required him to expand the boundaries of current language. It is a project fraught with danger; one in which it is almost impossible to succeed.

Evelyn asks himself in the final chapter of this two-thousand-page tome what it is that has driven him to undertake the writing of a work that must surely remain unread and unpublished. He likens the 'game' that he is playing with language to the 'game' that the body plays with consciousness. The body's 'game' includes the incitement to eat and drink (hunger and thirst) to rest (sleep) and to procreate and stimulate (sex). He regards pain as one of the games that the body plays with consciousness. He feels that one can concede defeat (masochism) or fight back (as in pranayama yoga). He cites other weapons like drugs but sees that more as an attack on the body than a mode of defence. Playing the language game is a more sophisticated defence mechanism.

The language game is a structured response by consciousness to the body's demands. He asks the question if Juvenal's *'mens sana in corpore sano'* is true, then does this mean that an unhealthy body or one in chronic pain must cause the mind to be unhealthy? His conclusion is that if this were true, and since most of humankind suffers pain of varying types and degrees, then as a species we are systematically certain to suffer from unhealthy minds. His response is that the fight back must include a full understanding of the enemy we face – pain. So, he sees his book as a weapon.

Why was this book written at all? Various critics, who could not have read it, assumed that this is the crazed work of the greatest hypochondriac to have ever lived. This I doubt as Evelyn appears to have had an unusually high pain threshold. Of course, any reviewer must consider the opinion of the author as to why he has written his book. But I suspect that Evelyn's opinion can only be a partial explanation as to his motivation. His own experience of pain appears to be one of extreme sensitivity. He himself admits to loss of consciousness on many occasions caused by the intensity of pain. Perhaps his own mind was more affected by the ravages he withstood undergoing surgery than he would want to reveal even to himself. He scarcely refers to the final 'game' played by the body on consciousness. If death marks an end to consciousness, any pathologist will tell you that it does not mark the end of the body. Its final decomposition usually takes a great deal of time unless incinerated in an accident or crematorium. If Evelyn's authorship means anything in that final battle, it is to carry some of his experiences whilst conscious into future generations long after his own death. Unfortunately, however, his written style is so opaque and difficult to fathom that this will be an unlikely result. The 'Compendium of Pain' is likely to remain as a huge undertaking sitting on this reviewer's shelves in folio form in the four boxes Evelyn sent me. The boxes, ironically, are shaped like coffins.

TRANS

It all started with that damned National Quiz Competition. Most people regarded it as light entertainment although the monetary prize attracted several young people who formed teams, hoping to win enough to pay off their student debts. The questions covered a wide span of general knowledge, but the objections raised concerning the choice of the final question hit the national press and social media in an entirely unpredictable way.

It was random chance that the final two teams happened to contain only men. Dozens of teams had competed with about as many females as male contestants. The fact that one team were all old men and the other all undergraduates made it look like a battle between generations. But this was entirely fortuitous and only became an issue when the final, deciding question was read out.

'What connects Perry Mason with Ironsides?' was met with puzzled looks amongst the undergraduates who had heard of neither. All four of the pensioners pressed their buzzers to answer as all of them had watched the two tv series when younger and remembered that Raymond Burr was the actor who had played both parts.

"UNFAIR" headlined one national newspaper the following day. And soon, supporters of the defeated team demanded that pensioners be banned for the next competition if questions were going to refer to "obscure, ancient history".

"Why should old fogeys with plenty of money in their pensions be allowed to compete when youngsters are struggling to make ends meet?"

"Why should we regard these fogeys as 'men' at all? They don't work like us; their biology has already changed irrevocably. Perhaps they were men at birth but, by now, they should be seen as fogeys – a totally different class of competitor."

With the leadership of those who had been defeated in the final round, a campaign group was formed. A journalist, initially with a clear touch of irony, called them "trans-exclusionary radical males". His original article stated that trans-exclusionary radical males (or 'terms') rejected the right of fogeys to compete in Quiz Competitions because "they are not really men as they have 'transed' into fogey with all the advantages of age and knowledge. This is very unfair to young men who cannot compete with this type of biological advantage."

The furore that ensued as those who had been caught up in the dispute over people who had transitioned from one gender to another became muted when the 'terms' pointed out that whilst less than half a percent of the UK population may or may not be affected by this earlier dispute, nearly twenty percent were over 65.

"Why should we tolerate the imposition that we young people have to put up with? We not only have our hopes and dreams crushed when competing for money, we find ourselves paying out billions on fogeys. £124 billion on State pensions and about half of the £176 billion we spend on health services (let alone social care) we pay out on fogeys."

On tv, one of the defeated team denounced the system with these words. "Our money is ripped from our grasp by old fogeys who were contemporaries of Perry Mason and Ironsides. About two hundred billion of our money – yes! OUR MONEY – as we are taxpayers now and they aren't! They take away 200 billion every year but, not satisfied with that, they snatch away the national quiz competition prize. It's not fair!"

In parliament, the rights of young men became a party-political issue as so-called 'terms' wanted to define men to exclude those "who had been born male but, once over 65, clearly could no longer be defined as the same." One party had researchers identifying more precisely how much of the government's money was spent on "those who had 'transed' and were no longer male but fogey." One minister was heard to question whether it was even legal to pay money out to those who could not fill in their census question correctly as 'fogey' did not appear as an option.

We all know how this entire dispute impacted upon the parallel debate concerning the right to euthanasia. Encouraging those who previously had regarded themselves as men to question whether they had an identity recognised in society became an issue at the following election. Led by what had become a new movement ('terms' and their followers that included millions of women hoping to rid themselves of the burden of supporting old men), their landslide victory at the polls gave the new administration all the legitimacy they needed to build the gleaming new euthanasia centres.

I can only apologise and wish that I had never dreamt up the questions to be asked at the quiz competition.

KWAME

Kwame's mother refused to let her son die. The hospital doctors told her that they could see little chance of him surviving, but she insisted on taking him home. The family lived in squalid conditions, and it is remarkable that Kwame fought through his early childhood. I was called to attend to the baby only days after his birth.

The deformity was unique. Short, stubby legs and an elongated body gave Kwame a strange appearance. What was even more peculiar was the perilously feeble spinal column and rubbery bones that encased his abdomen. I recommended that the baby be wrapped in thick towelling to prevent his body from being accidentally bent. When he was older, we had a special plastic exoskeleton made so that he could walk without endangering his fragile frame.

My patients were all black or coloured. As an Indian doctor, I was not permitted to practise on white people. So, when I reported Kwame's unusual condition, the government authority's reaction was at first disbelief. "Are you trying to make a name for yourself?" was how the Chief Medical Officer responded on the phone. I assured him that Kwame's disability was exactly as I had described it.

When Kwame's mother attempted to gain some support for her son, the authorities were less than helpful. One officer cited the opinion of the hospital doctor who had recommended that Kwame be allowed to die soon after birth. "You took responsibility when you snatched him away from the hospital, now you can solve your own problems."

There were many occasions when I was called on to attend to the little patient. But always I was met with those clear, determined eyes of a boy who would never give up his fight for life.

At school, Kwame discovered the pains of being bullied. He was an easy target as he hobbled along within his plastic frame, using his crutches to move at any speed. His arms, however, were disproportionately powerful in compensation for his malformed legs. Bullies who got within reach of his fists were soon dissuaded from tackling him head-on. But his time at school was mainly unhappy.

It was me who suggested that Kwame might benefit from exercising in a swimming pool. The fact that there were no swimming facilities in the shantytown did not deter his mother. She took him down to the rocky coast and lowered him carefully into the sea. She reported the effect to me the next day. I assumed that she was exaggerating in the way that parents often do when speaking of their child's achievements. It was another year before I witnessed Kwame's swimming abilities myself.

The school had been granted access to a rundown swimming pool to hold their sports day. Swimming and diving were not as popular as football; but the head teacher had decided that both girls and boys could demonstrate their skills in the water. He did not believe that girls could play football. I was invited to attend so that I could be one of the community leaders who gave out the prizes.

The event was noisy, and everyone cheered their friends as they plied their way through the water. The pool was only twenty-five metres long, and some competitors even found that quite a distance! But it was all good fun until the event where Kwame featured. It was billed as a one hundred metre freestyle race – four lengths of the pool. The well-muscled bodies of the older boys stood erect and waiting for the starting whistle. On the end lane, reserved for youngsters or disabled swimmers, Kwame balanced precariously on the edge of the pool. The whistle blew and Kwame flopped into the water, already ten metres behind the big boys. Then the most amazing transformation occurred. His strange, dangerously flexible body shot through the water. It undulated like a fish. He reached the end of the pool at the same time as the older swimmers. By the time they had completed the second lap, Kwame had nearly finished the third. He reached the final stretch before any of the others were halfway through the third. As he dragged himself out, he was greeted by an astounded silence.

My written application to the country's Olympic Committee was supported by the head teacher. In it I gave an accurate account of what I had seen and requested that a representative of the sport's governing body come and see for himself what Kwame could do. The response was odd. It was a photocopied set of rules for swimming freestyle with notes beside them.

It began:

1. A forward start shall be used. (Note: did you check the kid was facing the front?)

2. In an event designated freestyle, the swimmer may swim any style, except that in a medley relay or an individual medley event, freestyle means any style other than butterfly, breaststroke, or backstroke. Some part of the swimmer must break the surface of the water throughout the race, except it shall be permissible for the swimmer to be completely submerged during the turn and for a distance of not more than 15 meters (16.4 yards) after the start and each turn. By that point the head must have broken the surface. (Note: did you check if the boy came up before 15 meters had been swum underwater?)

3. Upon completion of each length the swimmer must touch the wall (Note: who checked if the boy cheated?)

4. The swimmer shall have finished the race when any part of his person touches the wall after completing the prescribed distance (Note: did anyone bother timing the kid?)

I wrote back explaining that the swimming pool was not a 50-metre pool. It was just a small one that had been set aside for a school sports day. No one had been taking timings and the Olympic rules were not being enforced by officials. However, I suggested that if an official could oversee a demonstration of the extraordinary swimming talent of the young boy, it was likely that he would witness the breaking of world records. After about a month, a letter arrived at my cramped surgery. It informed me that it was not in the child's nor the country's best interests to build up the hopes of a youngster. "We prefer to let young talent from the black community mature before we take it too seriously."

I was irate at the way Kwame was being overlooked by an official whom I suspected might never have even dived into a swimming pool. I wrote again, this time with a copy to the President's office. I hoped that when the official saw that the President himself was going to be involved, Kwame might be taken more seriously. So, I was gratified when a week later the letter arrived inviting Kwame and myself to the great 50-metre pool in the centre of the city.

I had never been to the Olympic sized pool. It was reserved for serious, white swimmers during the day and recreational swimmers who would zoom up in their 4-wheel drive vehicles in the evenings. Kwame was told to be ready to swim at five o'clock in the morning. He came with his mother and me, and we walked into the entrance at half past four. There was no one there, but the pool was open. The boy got changed and stood in his frame, bleary-eyed but ready to launch himself into the pool at five o'clock. By half past five, it was clear that no one was going to arrive to see the wonder child perform. He was shivering with cold and asked if he could swim, just to get warm. I said I was sure that it would be allowed, and I took out my stopwatch to see if I could time him – even if this would not be official.

His first fifty metres were covered in twelve seconds. I knew that this nearly halved the world record. But that was not the end of it. He just continued swimming. His next hundred metres only took him twenty-five seconds. Then he just carried on swimming with scarcely a flicker of fatigue. After two hundred metres he broke the world record by nearly a minute, and four hundred metres by two minutes! His mother called him out and asked if he felt tired. He smiled and said that he felt warmer now. Then he asked when the Olympic man was coming. No one came. We waited until seven o'clock then made our way back. I had my surgery and Kwame had school. His mother was philosophical about our disappointment. "This is much as I expected. We are never taken seriously." I was much less sanguine and felt personally affronted by the callousness of the official. I began composing a haughty letter to the President himself, with a copy to the official.

Perhaps I should not have included the times that I had recorded in the letter. But I felt that my account highlighting the amazing feats achieved by the boy was certain to bring forward the day when he would be brought to the world's attention. The silence that followed my letter ought to have warned me that my expectations were unlikely to be met. But I ploughed on with my campaign to have Kwame's talent recognised. I asked the head teacher if he would organise a petition in support of Kwame being allowed to compete in an adult competition. His discomfort at the request ought to have acted as yet another indication to me that my obsession was going to cause me trouble.

The charge brought against me was a shock. I was arrested and brought to court. 'Falsification of official documents' it said on the charge sheet. "What official documents am I meant to have falsified?" I asked. I had always been extremely meticulous in my medical record keeping. I could not imagine where I had slipped up. In court I discovered that the document in question was my report to the Olympic Committee where incorrect timings were provided against a swimmer (Kwame was not even named). The judge took one look at the times I had provided, compared them with the current world records and, without another word, found me guilty. I was told that I could no longer practise medicine as it would be impossible to grant a licence to a man who falsified official records.

Kwame's mother told me that her son disappeared after another round of school bullying. He was called a freak, a fish, and a lot worse. He had not come home but had been seen propelling himself towards the beach. His frame and school bag were found abandoned beside the water's edge. A ferryboat lookout did report seeing what looked like a human swimming far out to sea that evening: but then he dismissed the sighting as the speed at which the figure was travelling far outstripped any that was possible by a person.

I retired the day that Nelson Mandela became President. Kwame's mother celebrated Mandela's victory. "Perhaps Kwame will return now we have our man in charge!" she said to me. I smiled and said that would be wonderful. I sometimes wonder whether Kwame perished far out to sea or whether he may have found more congenial company with a dolphin colony. As for me, my final years were spent trying to keep my family on an income earned as a swimming pool attendant.

THE TREE IN THE PARK

The realisation crept up on James. He had been aware, for many years, that we had been polluting Earth. He knew all about what people called "climate change". He felt he was doing his bit in preserving the health of the planet by recycling his plastic bottles, tin cans and driving an electric car. Of course, he was not stupid and did not believe for one moment that his contribution had any significance beyond his own deluded conscience. But he continued to build these 'green' habits into his daily routine in the hope that if millions of others did the same, then his grandchildren might enjoy a better life.

His wife, Jane, had joined a women's "collective" that campaigned against abortion. She argued fiercely that life begins at conception, so termination of any fetus was akin to murder. James had listened to the opposing arguments around the rights of women to make decisions about their own bodies and, although he said nothing to Jane, he was genuinely conflicted over the issue.

"You are an arborealist," Jane explained to her uncertain husband. "You know very well that a tree begins life long before it spreads its branches and grows leaves."

But James argued that there were always strong reasons why a tree might need to be chopped down.

"That is no argument," Jane responded. "Humans kill each other and argue that there are good reasons why they should. War seems to be a permanent feature of society throughout the world. But that doesn't make it right."

James always felt confused when arguing with Jane. She always seemed to be so sure of herself whereas he quickly got lost in any debate that did not appear to have a very clear and uncontentious outcome.

Jane was away with her collective making forceful representations to well-known political leaders and, more importantly, to the tv cameras and assorted podcasters, bloggers, and journalists whom they regarded as their audience. He had a job to assess the health and viability of a copse of tress that had grown close together in an urban park. He was being asked to make a professional judgement as to whether the trees would be able to grow better if they did not interfere with each other's access to sunlight. A company, owned by the brother of the Council's leader, would be paid to remove the trees, and would be paid again by the purchaser of the wood. But the local community group wanted the trees left exactly as they stood.

He entered the park armed with nothing but his phone on which he could take photographs, a very long tape measure (that he hardly ever used), and a notepad and pencil to undertake any preliminary observations. There was no one else in the park apart from a couple of early morning joggers. The sun had just risen, and a quiet breeze was shuffling the abundant leaves of the giant oak that overhung the pathway. It was at that moment that he suddenly saw the oak in a completely different way – as an impressive and complex, living entity.

Later, he was too tongue-tied to explain what he had seen to his wife – annoyed at what she saw as his inability to grasp what was important and what was not. He saw the leaves' slow movements as if in a choreographed dance with the air, itself cavorting to the powerful music of the sun's heat. "All life," he said to Jane, "is really nothing but a massive planetwide dance with the sun."

"Exactly!" she exclaimed. "Now you can see why abortion is so wrong."

"But all dance has twists and turns, pauses and sudden bursts of energy. Dancers drop out, others join. The sun is not particular about its partners."

"Good God, James! You really do talk a load of rubbish at times."

He told her that he was recommending that the trees in the park should be left exactly how they were. But Jane said the oak overhanging the path should be cut down as it interfered with where her collective undertook their sponsored runs.

THE TAILORS

When I knew the Tailors, I saw them as a typical hardworking suburban family. They lived in an outlying, run-down area in south Chicago. John Tailor worked as a foreman in the local engineering factory and his wife, Jane, was active in her church and the charity shop supporting children with disabilities. Their son, Robert, and daughter, Linda, attended the same local school and, although neither were distinguished academically, both enjoyed success in sports. Linda was captain of the girls' hockey team; and Robert's unusual height made him a popular member of the basketball team.

When Robert – who never normally complained about discomfort – reported an ache around his navel, Jane became concerned. After a few days, the pain low down on the right side of his belly became sharp. Their doctor immediately diagnosed appendicitis and had him admitted to hospital.

In the hospital, John and Jane assumed that their surgeon (that was me) would remove Robert's appendix. But I explained that this would not be necessary as a course of antibiotics would almost certainly resolve the pain being caused by the inflamed appendix.

"But what if the pain persists?" Jane asked.

"Then we can operate," I replied. "But, meanwhile, the latest research suggests that if we can retain the appendix, this might bring benefits. The appendix appears to help us with storing good gut bacteria and the tailbone does have important muscles, tendons, and ligaments attached to it."

"I thought the appendix was just a leftover from when we had tails," John said.

I think I automatically adopted the pose used at seminars for medical students and said: "it's hard to say how fast it may take for some vestigial features like the appendix to change or disappear. We would have to predict mutations that change the expression of the structure, reproductive patterns of individuals and populations, as well as environmental conditions in the future. We just don't know which traits will be a liability or which structures will be advantageous in an environment so influenced by human activity and technology."

"I'm sorry," Jane interrupted, "I have no idea what you are talking about. What are you saying?" I dropped the lecturing stance that I had unthinkingly adopted when remembering that I was not at the University.

"Oh! I am sorry. I was saying that you are right about what the appendix may have evolved from. But some of the benefits of retaining the appendix might be useful in the future. So, if Robert can keep it for the moment by having the pain stopped by treating the inflammation with an antibiotic, then he may also keep the benefits as he grows older."

Jane looked at John to see how her husband was reacting. He looked back at her, shrugged his shoulders and said: "Well if your professional opinion is that Robert should try to keep his appendix, we will go along with that for the moment. But if our son's pain persists, we will insist that you remove the appendix."

I was happy as the antibiotic prescription was working within a couple of days. Robert's pain died down, and he went back to playing in the school basketball team. But within days, I was confronted with the Tailors again. This time it was Robert's sister, Linda, who was exhibiting the signs of appendicitis. As the antibiotics had worked with Robert, I thought the same might be best for Linda. After taking time for prayer and reflection, Jane talked to John about what she believed to be divine affirmation of the antibiotic pathway. They agreed with my recommendation and, sure enough, within a fortnight, Linda was back playing on the hockey field.

Robert was surprised but not really bothered when a bump appeared at the base of his spine. Linda, however, was very self-conscious as the signs of a tail growing behind her back became increasingly visible. John and Jane, as adoring parents, could not conceive how what they regarded as a strange aberration could possibly bring benefits to their lovely kids. Jane's pastor, Father Ignatius, went into a trancelike state and declared that any hint of a tail had demonic implications. So, Jane demanded that the offending appendages be surgically removed.

I will admit that I was excited by what I described as a "unique devolution" about which I wanted to publish an academic study. However, I realised that if I were to gain any plaudits from my professional peers, I would have to handle the parents carefully as removing the rapidly developing tails would see the end of any interest from my medical colleagues. I held an honorary professorship in faraway Philadelphia and managed to persuade the anxious parents that a more precise examination could be undertaken with the facilities in Philadelphia. I lied to Jane by claiming that I had experienced a revelation whilst at prayer that a city of "brotherly love" would bring about a divinely ordained conclusion to their situation.

So, despite pronouncements from Father Ignatius warning against such a trip, Linda and her mother accompanied me on a hurriedly arranged flight from Chicago to Philadelphia. John and Robert remained at home. Before we flew, I had a chat with Father Ignatius whom I had known for many years. He had long ago given all his considerable inherited wealth away to establish the charity where Jane volunteered. He was an influential and easy-going leader of our community who could enjoy a joke whilst praying for all our souls. I told him that I had far better facilities in Philadelphia, but he remained unconvinced of my motives.

Linda's "tail" was becoming so pronounced that it could no longer be hidden beneath standard clothing. My team undertook a range of examinations and took samples for analysis. Jane demanded to know what the outcome of the work was going to be. But before I could discuss options and prognoses with the mother and daughter, I rushed an account of the findings to the Philadelphia University Journal of Medicine with my name featuring prominently at the head of the article. A journalist working for the local newspaper seized on what had been written and produced a sensational account about the Tailors. Jane was horrified when the first thing that she knew of it was when 'The Tail of Two Cities' appeared on the front page.

She phoned home to find John and Robert overwhelmed with paparazzi jostling to obtain photographs of the son's appendage. I said that the journal where I had published was where fellow professionals could assess and evaluate options with me so that we could find the very best way forward for the patients. I was as appalled as they were by the gutter press and its depiction of their condition although Jane was clearly unconvinced of my sincerity.

"So, what are you going to do about it?!" she demanded. "Can you remove Linda's tail so that she can go back to growing up as a normal girl?"

"It seems that the issue is not as simple as that," I explained. "Removal might be dangerous as the appendage seems to be organically integrated into your daughter's central nervous system. She appears to be growing this as a natural development so, even if it were cut off, it would probably grow back but bring with it a multitude of infection issues that are being avoided by allowing the growth to proceed without interference."

Back in Chicago, young Robert told his father that he did not regard having a tail as a grave disadvantage. "It doesn't hurt, and it has already grown long enough for me to grasp chair legs with it. It almost acts as a third arm but without the fingers!" John was quite impressed by his son's assertive announcements and decided that he was in no position to oppose the young man's wishes. Curiosity amongst journalists was waning ... it had become old news very fast. The one exasperating hanger-on who seemed to want to follow the young man was dealt with harshly by Robert himself.

One evening, as he was returning home from school, the stalker confronted Robert with a demand to show him his tail. "You mean you want me to undress in front of you?" Robert asked. He said this in a very loud voice as he could see that a policewoman was standing at the corner of the street talking with two patrol men in their police car. The stalker was blithely unaware of their presence behind him. Taking the question as some sort of assent, the man began to strip Robert and continued even though Robert kept shouting for him to stop. By the time that Robert was down to his underclothes and the stalker had his camera phone clicking furiously, the policewoman had her hand firmly on the cameraman's shoulder. But before she could arrest him and place him with her colleagues in the police car, Robert revealed his nearly full-length tail and swept the man off his feet, tossing him several yards up the street – much to the policewoman's amazement.

"Thank you for saving me," Robert said as the patrol men joined the policewomen to take the stalker into custody.

"You're a freak!" he shouted at Robert. "And you have assaulted me. I demand the police arrest you!"

"Clear case of self-defence," the police said as they took the man away.

"I quite admire how you handled the situation," the policewoman told him.

Robert reported the incident to John when he got home. His father was impressed by Robert's fast-developing ability to use the tail as a formidable defensive weapon. That evening, Jane and Linda returned home from Philadelphia and the Tailor family sat down together to decide how they were going to handle their uncertain future.

"Let us pray together" Jane said. But neither Robert nor John had any faith in appeals to Heaven.

"Your Father Ignatius seems to think I am some sort of demon," Robert said. "I do not want anything to do with him and his evangelical sect. I think you should leave them, mother, as I do not believe a word he says."

John was more tactful in questioning his wife's devotion but similarly sceptical of the priest's advice. Linda was too upset by what had been happening all around her to have an opinion about what her brother inaccurately called "a crazy monk". But she was shocked when her brother described the incident with his stalker. "Are there members of this church who would want me to strip in public so they could photograph my naked body?" she asked.

Jane was embarrassed to admit that when the identity of Robert's stalker was revealed, she recognised him as a devout member of Ignatius's church. The family agreed to take less heed of pronouncements from the church and to engage with me, the untrustworthy but knowledgeable surgeon.

That night, whilst they were all asleep, Father Ignatius felt compelled to undertake God's work by breaking into the house and shooting all the Tailors dead.

STREETS AHEAD

You may not approve of the unscrupulous set-up from which he became wealthy, but many of us have a quiet admiration for Gary's 'Streets Ahead' business.

He says that he first thought of the scheme when he read how a local council had responded after being ridiculed for living in an earlier age. A radio reporter had commented on how the little town had just one crossroad and no traffic lights. "Can you imagine a place that claims to be a town sporting zero traffic lights?" Within weeks, the town had responded by claiming that it had many crossroads (even though they were just intersections between quiet residential cul-de-sacs and tiny streets) and had purchased a dozen sets of traffic lights to manage where these intersections occurred.

Gary already had a stable but unremarkable trade in street furniture. Mostly this consisted of responding to local authorities wanting to remove outdated or irrelevant clutter from their roads. The cost of authority disposal was greater than the price Gary charged to remove it from the roadside. It was after he read about the town worried about its status because of the lack of traffic lights that Gary's diabolical scheme took shape.

His investment in an experienced team of journalists soon started paying dividends. Village after village, town after town, pilloried by the journalists for being so old-fashioned, reacted against the epithet "quaint and quiet" by buying redundant street furniture from Gary's stock. Disposal was no longer a cost; it was becoming the most profitable side of the business!

Hurriedly erected and rarely tested, the old but newly commissioned traffic lights were being filmed by his video journalist. Gary was parading his vintage sports car to reinforce the image of a rural town living in the past. Unfortunately, the traffic lights were green in all directions when the truck smashed into Gary as he was traversing the crossing.

The video of this tragic event is on sale from Streets Ahead.

RED HANDED

The crop was valuable. It had taken all year for the Kamzit plants to come to fruition. Careful soil management and constant surveillance to deter pests had brought about an excellent line of the new organism. After two years in the laboratory where the genetically altered plant had been cross fertilized with a wide variety of fruits with potential for organic development, the final lines in the locked greenhouses were ready for harvesting.

Despite anti-theft defences that were unheard of until the announcement of the crop's supposed benefits had been illegally leaked, the video of the thieves cutting the plants down and piling them onto their van was plain to see. The two guards' loyalty was immediately questioned even though they had suffered severe injuries. Both had been knocked unconscious: one was severely concussed and the other suffered long term brain damage. The police showed little interest in the theft – and not much more in the serious assault on the two men.

"There is not much we can do about tracing stolen fruit," the police sergeant said.

"This is not just ordinary fruit," Professor John Carey tried to explain. But the (admittedly fictitious) description of scientific benefits evinced little or no response.

The Zein Institute's investment subsidiary had spent considerable sums on the creation of the Kamzit and the employment of John Carey and his team. Karen Zein, Zein's Chief Executive, visited the greenhouses where Carey showed her what had taken place. She had a strong suspicion that the theft had been planned and carried out by men working for a rival company.

"I cannot prove that Delfont's were behind this," she told Carey. "But if you know any way we could trace what has happened to our crop, now is the time to take action before it is too late to save the plants."

"There is one problem with Kamzits that requires mechanical handling," he told Karen Zein. "But, for all the wrong reasons, it may prove to be of immense benefit in tracking the thieves."

He explained how the plant pods had to be extracted with precise robotic arms because the budding pods contained an indelible red filament from where the valuable cream could be extracted. In its raw state, the corrosive and brilliant crimson filaments could prove dangerous – even lethal – if in contact with human flesh.

When the Delfont gang were admitted to hospital, their hands were so badly damaged that two had hands amputated and two others had already lost fingers before any treatment could be started. Still, they denied knowing anything about the Kamzits, claiming that their condition was the result of an industrial accident within a Delfont factory. Again, the police seemed incapable of acting.

"There is no proof that these men were in your greenhouses," the Inspector who had eventually been assigned to the case explained. "We would have to acquire some evidence that links them to the greenhouse break-in and the attack on the two guards."

"If I were allowed to take a tiny sample of the skin, I would be able to prove that the damage could only have been done by our genetically modified plant."

"I am afraid that, unsurprisingly, access to their hands and their medical records has been denied."

"I think we need to take this to the press and make a big fuss on social media," Karen Zein announced before the Inspector. "Although Delfonts will not look good, I suspect the inaction of the police will look even worse."

The Inspector looked more anxious at this prospect. He was trained to be suspicious and now turned his attention to Carey.

"Tell me, why were you making such dangerous items? Are you licensed to manufacture weapons? Can I see any agreements that you have with the authorities which would allow you to grow these monstrous plants?"

Carey looked at Karen and laughed. "I think you should tell the Inspector why Zein is so interested in Kamzit."

Karen took a deep breath and started a lengthy monologue concerning how manufacturing licenses were gained in her industry. She kept until the end before describing what the intended outcome was although she swore the policeman to secrecy before divulging the aim.

"But that is not what the papers reported as benefits!" he exclaimed. "They just said that the fruit could be made into the tastiest fat reducing food on the market."

"Well, we had to give some reason for the unprecedented security arrangements. But if we had announced the real reasons for Kamzit, we believe that we could have been exposed to sabotage, political protest and a far greater degree of unwanted attention."

"We need to get the stolen plant shoots and pods returned," Carey said. "If they remain away from our regenerative resolvent for more than a couple of days, they could break down and become even more dangerous."

Finally, it seemed that the Inspector grasped the seriousness of the situation. He called together the police unit and explained to the Chief of Police that additional officers were required as a matter of urgency.

"And when you find them, do not touch. Just call Carey and he will send the specialist handling equipment."

A warrant to search the Delfont factories and storage facilities quickly uncovered where the unfortunate thieves had deposited the Kamzits. Carey had his team collect them and reposition them back in the greenhouses before they degenerated; and Karen Zein engaged her legal team to take out a prosecution against Delfonts. All seemed to have worked out for the best (apart from the men who had literally found their swag too hot to handle).

But that was only the beginning of the story for Karen Zein and John Carey. Once the pods had been harvested and treated, the fruit was ready to be ingested. But the side effects were impossible to predict. They could be different for men and women: so, they decided that one man and one woman should act as guinea pigs. Instead of launching a standard drugs trial with volunteers, Karen Zein and John Carey volunteered to be the first to trial the fruit.

The results have never been repeated. John Carey believes that the way that the pods were treated when stolen altered them in ways that have been impossible to replicate. The chromosomal alteration for both him and Karen was irreversible. As we all know now, the pods accidentally spilt within the Delfonts factory turned out to have all the necessary characteristics required to create what we have on the market today. The Delfont pills, that they called 'Zines', were the first mass produced gender altering tablet whose dramatic sex-changing effects were reversible simply by taking another Zine.

Karen (now called Karl) Zein and John (now called Joan) Carey argued in court that the massive profits made by Delfonts through the sale of Zines should rightfully be paid over to the Zein Corporation as the creator of Kamzits. But the judge (whose family members it was subsequently discovered were major shareholders in Delfonts) ruled against them. Since then, both have written extensively about the dangers of undertaking sex change procedures without a full understanding of the context within which we live and work.

In the past decade since Zines became freely available, the large number of women who did not want to bear children found that although sex reversal back to being a woman was easy, the effect of Zines made childbearing very problematic. They found that after transitioning into being men, there were significant differences that they displayed against men who had been born as men. On the other hand, men who had transitioned into being women were very like them and very different from those born as women. Most recently, government legal enactments have cleared the way for the formal recognition of three genders: male, female and 'zines'

Karl Zein and Joan Carey now insist that any official document requiring the applicant to declare their gender, 'zine' must be provided as an option. They have both published studies purporting to show that zines demonstrate greater ability in creative arts, scientific innovation and mental agility than both men and women. Both have been subjected to an avalanche of online abuse as well as threats to their physical safety from men and women of all political persuasions. Because of the abuse, there are many Zines who refuse to admit that they belong to this third gender. But they are easily distinguished; their hands are red.

GLINE

It seems that the Glines have been observing Earth for longer than humans have been around. Their interest in our planet only grew for one reason. According to the top military minds of our generation, this could only have been because of our development of Caesar Rays that could destroy entire armies from cunningly positioned satellite gunships. But when Lobin, whom our enemies labelled a "gung-ho dictator", decided to turn Caesar Rays towards the galactic cloud apparently housing Gline positions, he learnt to his and our cost that it was not this that interested them. The Ray's instant deflection back to its source decimated much of the military establishment that had been lovingly grown by our esteemed leader. The destruction was blamed upon homegrown saboteurs, but we all know it was the Glines who had decided to teach us a lesson.

The way that Gline contact had been established should have given a clue to the focus of their interest. When the complex patterns of signals were picked up, there were numerous attempts to decipher their meaning. The men and women tasked with decoding reported a feeling of warmth and affection pervading the otherwise clinically cold, hygienic laboratories in which they worked. Their decoding computer units trembled as they extracted snatches of linguistic output: but most decoding machines hummed and emitted what sounded like birdsong rather than intelligible words.

It was the Gline's apparent ignoring of our attempts to communicate verbally which made Lobin and others like him infer that Glines had ill intentions that they were hiding through silence or gibberish. After the elimination of Lobin's capacity to wage Caesar Ray war, no other nation followed his lead. An Australian team broadcast into space a wide variety of pictorial imagery from ancient aboriginal cave paintings to ultra-modern conceptual creations. They were rewarded by non-visual responses, but the wave patterns seemed to make the building where they worked vibrate. It was not until a Chinese team played a recording of a traditional folk song accompanied by a virtuoso guzheng player that the Gline response came back with an astonishing display of orchestral sound – but with instrumentation unlike anything that we used on Earth. The Chinese team shared the recording with other astronomy teams around the world and their shared opinion was that Gline culture had evolved to communicate through music.

"Perhaps they will like our latest pop songs and dance music" media outlets proclaimed who, also, happened to own the rights to play and distribute these mass-produced items. But Gline response to having this blasted out through space was muted. As the Chinese folk song had stimulated a response, other folk melodies from around the world were tried but with only limited success. Eventually, the virtuoso performance on the guzheng was identified as being the focus of their interest. And so it proved when recordings by the top pianists and violinists performing recognised masterpieces brought forth an avalanche of Gline soundscapes that matched the virtuosity of the world's greatest players.

Without any apparent linguistic communication system, our cleverest analysts were at a loss as to how Gline civilisation had evolved. Their technology appeared to be so many centuries more advanced than Earth's that we were unable to understand answers to the most fundamental questions we asked. How do you travel around the Universe? How do you procreate? Even, "what does a Gline look like?"

After a couple of months, the screen on an American astronomer's desk flickered into life – even though he had not turned it on. There was an image whose authenticity many have since questioned. "This must be a trick. Why do Americans always think they have to lead on major breakthroughs? We don't believe any of it." These were standard responses around the rest of the world, but the image looked like a female human being, albeit one with almost superhuman characteristics. She spoke in perfect English and explained that Gline interest had been sparked by some of the latest recordings of music by Bach, Mozart, Beethoven, Prokofiev, and Olivier Messiaen. Other composers were of intense interest, but Gline musical leadership had identified four or five specific recordings that they valued. Then she explained that Gline individuals communicate with one another through musical imagery. "We find this to be far more comprehensive in setting out how and why we think or feel rather than the ancient system that we once used that you call spoken language."

The astonished astronomer had asked the name of the female addressing them. What sounded like human laughter was accompanied by an explanation that there was no female speaking to them, only an image that the Gline had created together with an attempt to communicate in a clumsy foreign language so that humans could try to grasp a little about Gline culture. "What do you really look like?" was met with a blank screen.

Lobin's response to the Gline's apparent love of fine music was to have scores of leading performers and composers imprisoned. They were tried in courts whose judges had been appointed by Lobin. They were accused of being in secret communication with Glines using music that Lobin had decided should be banned. Their guilt was decided prior to their court appearance. To emphasise the message, Lobin had a concert grand piano ceremonially destroyed with axes and televised on the evening news. The piano was declared to have been the secret communication medium used to send the Glines messages. Lobin's henchmen whose military hardware had been destroyed when they had attempted to Caesar Ray the Glines decided to hunt down musicians and music teachers. One old lady who had taught the piano to preschool children died when Lobin's mob broke into her house.

Opponents of Lobin who had fled abroad appealed for help. But he had provided no pretext for others to intervene in the internal running of the country. Funds were raised to support the families of imprisoned musicians although it is doubtful that much got through to the intended recipients. Music in support of 'Rebels

Against Lobin' (R.A.L.) filled the airways and was fed through the Internet to keep up the spirits of those committed to R.A.L.. But Lobin had much social media shut down and foreign radio and tv stations had their signals jammed. The Caesar Ray catastrophe had taught him to focus his violent attentions only upon human adversaries.

Gline intervention arrived in ways that Lobin found difficult to contain. In response to a German broadcast with outstanding performers playing famous concertos for violin and orchestra, the Gline responded with what we now believe was their version of a concert. It was received by radio stations on every continent, and, despite Lobin's best efforts, nothing could prevent their music being heard by anyone with a radio. The seriously catchy tune that concluded the Gline performance was whistled and sung by children in every country – including ours and there seemed that Lobin could do nothing about it. R.A.L. even set revolutionary words to the theme. It became their anthem so Lobin ordered that anyone singing it in public should be shot.

There was huge controversy over the circumstances surrounding the death of our leader. Lobin made many enemies and being human, of course he made mistakes. But he achieved a level of economic growth that benefitted much of our population and gained the unswerving support of our religious authorities who claimed he was a "true patriot". In elections, he usually took over ninety nine percent of the votes – an astonishing achievement unequalled anywhere else in the world. Enemies abroad claimed he ran a corrupt dictatorship – but he said that they were just envious of his achievements. There was no one with him when he died so there were no witnesses to what happened. When his personal assistant arrived in the morning, the house servants opened the door and let him go into the private apartment to present Lobin with documents that needed his signature. When there was no response to his request to enter, the head butler was called to open the door with his electronic key. On entering, they found Lobin dead, in bed, wearing earphones playing live music.

Despite opposition from the military authorities, most of our imprisoned musicians have now been released. Intriguingly, the generals in charge of the army were persuaded to take no action against even the most rebellious of musicians by their own military band members. R.A.L. disbanded and the forthcoming election looks as if the party containing the most hardline religious leaders may not have enough support to gain more than just a couple of seats in our parliament. The leader of the most popular party, and the one that has garnered massive support from well-wishers around the world, is a well-known clarinettist who used to perform in the city's jazz clubs before being imprisoned by our late leader. The one great disappointment since Lobin's strange death has been the absolute silence from the Glines as if they are no longer there.

DREAM VIEWERS

Hailed as the greatest breakthrough in psychology – indeed, the greatest breakthrough in all biological science – the invention and eventual mass distribution of

Dream Viewers (DVs) seemed a revolution in how we understand ourselves. The simple projection onto the DV headpiece of whatever a sleeper was dreaming initially brought significant benefits to doctor/patient relationships where the patient was suffering from any form of trauma. The ability to view how the patient was internalising their experience as an externally recorded video permitted much faster diagnoses and even a viewable record of progress once treatment had started.

Mass distribution of DVs was driven by the belief that the item posed no danger to the public. It was regarded as a wonderful recreational item creating "deep" imagery suitable for self-reflection or discussion. DV Company profits soared as the patented item made cheap, unreliable copies impossible to market. Several artists used DVs as the basis their work although, it was noted, that few seemed to match the impact of images painted by Dali or Chagall who lived years before DVs were invented.

Only when the company began networking DV outputs worldwide did other businesses start paying to log into the DV network, hoping to discover common images that could, perhaps, be used as the basis for advertising. Soon, as many psychologists predicted, the imagery that overran marketing campaigns featured a remarkable display of what Carl Gustav Jung would have recognised as archetypal images that pervade all cultures. DV share price reached heights that its directors could hardly believe. It had become the most valuable business in the world: and yet the real power of DVs had not even become apparent.

Some say that the feedback loop was discovered entirely by chance. Certainly no one in the DV research team would admit that this was what they were seeking. But its impact made everything that had occurred initially dwindle into insignificance once the loop was instituted. Ensuring that no one else could access the loop, DV began feeding imagery into the system. Just as an experiment, they tried images that "suggested" how a small country's electorate should vote. The distributed imagery was strictly aimed at those who were identified as voters. After the election, DV monitors reported that the opposition party won a completely unexpected victory, overturning a massive government majority simply because the DV loop had such a dramatic effect upon the subconscious minds of those registered to vote.

DV directors recognised that this could open a far mor lucrative area for their business than mere recreational users and psychiatric patients. Product advertising would be dominated by DV imagery, purchased at a high price from their company. Political campaigns could forget all about tv advertising, pamphlets, door knocking and newspaper coverage. All that mattered was whether your side had purchased more DV imagery than your opponents to target especially undecided voters.

The murder of the Johnson brothers, who owned just over fifty percent of DV shares, began the terrible spiral down from which we have only just been shown how we might recover. At first Sandy Beach, who owned a third of the shares, was suspected. She had made approaches to the Johnsons with a view to buying a sixth of their stake so that she and the Johnsons would be equal in terms of ownership and decision-making powers. But Sandy seemed an unlikely assassin and her lifelong adherence to a particularly pious Buddhist sect and her secluded life in the ashram even made her contact with the outside world quite tenuous.

Attention of the authorities turned to groups who were regarded as "left wing" and had often voiced opposition to what they saw as the malign influence of DV upon democratic ideals. They asserted that the institute of the loop effectively undermined the foundation upon which all democracies depend, the capacity for voters to make informed and dispassionate decisions about who best represented their views and best defended the lives of themselves, their children, grandchildren and the wider community. Instead, these groups believed that the company had, in effect, sold elections to whoever paid most. But, again, the leaders of these groups were seen by the police as being long on speech and publications, but hardly active when it came to direct action unless you counted street demonstrations and rallies as platforms from which to launch a professionally orchestrated assassination.

The precision and almost military planning of the operation brought former soldiers under suspicion. The Johnsons had employed a dedicated set of bodyguards whose loyalty seemed indisputable. But still, all were questioned, and their movements fully accounted for. One retired general was well-known for what were regarded as "reactionary views" and had frequently expressed the view that society would be much better off if DV ceased to exist. However, although in his time there is no doubt that he could have conceived and carried out the operation, he was a hundred and one when the murders took place. He lived in a nursing home and received no visitors as all his family had since died.

Without the guiding hands of the Johnson brothers, the operations of DV continued without any restraints. There had been precious little attempt to keep the worst excesses of the loop under control before, but without the Johnsons as gatekeepers, anyone could buy absolutely anything to circulate on the loop. Attempts by various governments to restrict the coverage of the loop were largely unsuccessful as the loop spread without requiring cables, broadcasters, radio or tv transmitters or any of the old circuitry of the Internet. When the United National General Assembly voted overwhelmingly that DV as a company should be dissolved and the entire DV system closed down, no one seemed to know how or where to go to carry out such a decision. The Johnsons were dead, Sandy Beach seemed to have little or no control over the company's operation. The celebrated research team turned out to be a motley crew of individual developers residing in towns and villages across the globe with no apparent central point of command.

The company shares ceased trading by order of the American, Japanese, German, Chinese and Brazilian governments as they were quoted only on the New York, Tokyo, Frankfurt, Beijing and Sao Paulo exchanges. But still the loop appeared to be untouched. It seemed to have a life of its own quite apart from the parent company from which it had been spawned. Access to the loop was discovered to require no permission from DV, entry simply required the payment of a tiny sum into an account that the authorities were quick to close. But access was still gained simply by ordering payment even if this was never carried out.

Finally, Sandy Beach appeared before the cameras to make an announcement. It was broadcast throughout every continent and explained in simple terms what action was required. There was no reason to disbelieve her as carrying out what she said would leave her completely penniless.

"There is only one way to rid us of the curse of the DV loop. Carrying this out will make DV worthless and impossible to revive. It must be rejected universally; left unused for 24 hours, without anyone attempting to access. If you can all manage to contain your addiction to Dream Viewing, then we will be saved from its excesses. But if only one person breaks the 24-hour embargo, the loop will remain operational. That is the challenge. Can you all work together or will there aways be at least one person happy to destroy our civilisation and the lives of our children and grandchildren?"

CONVICT COLONY

Criminology lectures tend to be boring. The module I was studying in my sociology degree required attendance at a lecture by the Professor of Crime Statistical Analysis – an early morning commitment to which I was not looking forward.

The Professor was an old man and spoke more to himself than to the disparate group of students who had wandered across the campus to claim their attendance points. No one was really listening to his words and the drone in his voice seemed to register how unimportant he knew his contribution was to our education.

I perked up slightly when he challenged us to say what form of punishment could be established in a society where resources were communal and shared but if there were no such thing as prison. He described Moses leading Egyptian Jews into the Sinai desert as an example.

One bright spark responded that he thought that Australian aborigines had the best idea: stabbing offenders in the leg with a spear. The more serious the offence, the more damaging the injury. The Professor smiled at this suggestion but pointed out that incarceration was still an option for aboriginal communities whereas the Jews who had fled Egypt under Moses were in the desert. Stabbing offenders in the leg there would probably render them unable to survive so would, in effect, be a death sentence.

Gloria, my black girlfriend, was sitting beside me and showed off her knowledge of history when she suggested that an alternative had been tried in 18th and 19th century England where offenders were transported to Australia. The Professor looked sad as he described the likely experience of being incarcerated on a ship, then being dumped in an inhospitable land. "English convicts and African slaves at least had that in common," Gloria commented.

The old man nodded and still speaking more to himself than to the class, went on: "The phrase 'hell on Earth' must have come from those who sentenced me to a lifetime on this planet. At least where I come from, we don't spend vast amounts of time systematically killing one another. Earth is our convict colony ... I just wish I could go home before I die."

CHESHIRE CAT

Richard found it hard to accept that he would no longer see Sandra, his partner, wife, confidante, and lover of forty years. The trees surrounding their house whispered in the wind: perhaps he could hear the hushed sound of her name. The shapes of the twigs and branches evoked the curves of her smile – disappearing quickly like Alice's cheshire cat. But this was no wonderland: her absence made Richard struggle to catch his breath.

He had always known that one of them would go first, leaving the other to cope in the world alone. But it was the speed of the separation that had come as a surprise. He had always imagined that one would slowly fade, perhaps in a care home being tended by the survivor. Death would come as an expected conclusion: if great pain was being experienced, maybe even a welcome ending. But finding a finale that took only a couple of days provided no opportunity to prepare oneself. He found himself muttering, "it's not fair; we could not even say goodbye."

Neither of them had any time for the rituals of religion. But that did not stop the local vicar making a call. And, despite not being summoned, his presence helped Sandra in arranging Richard's funeral.

IT'S A WISE MAN WHO KNOWS HIS FATHER

It was only at the funeral of my dad that my mum told me the truth. "Listen," she whispered after all the mourners had gone. "Your dad was a wonderful husband. He might not have been the brightest man I've known, but he was certainly the strongest. He was so energetic, a true athlete. And even at fifty, he insisted on indulging in extreme sports. I did discourage him, but freefall paragliding was too much for him to resist."

"I understand," I replied. "So, he died doing the sport he loved." She nodded and looked at me. "Tell me," She started. "Have you ever wondered why your body was so unlike his?"

"I suppose it was just bad luck." She paused and took a deep breath. "Your dad was not actually your father," she announced. It took a little while for me to digest this news. After a moment I blurted out, "but you are my mother, aren't you?"

Yes, of course."

"So, who is my father?"

"Well, you know about my job."

"You work at the Tempo Foundation."

"Yes, I was appointed by the founder, Guru Mohindra. His legacy has been felt by many millions around the world. The Foundation is one of the wealthiest on the planet, so I am very busy nowadays. But it was not always so. Originally, I was one of the guru's students. His teaching was so revolutionary that no one believed his claims."

"Yes, I know he claimed that our perception of time was an illusion. He said that it was only one of several perceptions of which we are capable and that other perceptions could be engaged through meditation."

My mother looked surprised. "I didn't know you took an interest in his teachings. Anyway, I was his most devoted follower. I was only twenty-two when I had an affair with him just after I married your dad. Mohindra was your father, but your dad never knew."

I nodded, reflecting upon the many things I had never understood about my own body. "So was Mohindra as thin and weak as me?"

"He was very thin. I think that was due to the fasting he did whilst meditating. It was in those meditations that he told me that he could sense certain things in our future. Don't look surprised when I tell you that he claimed to be able to hear sounds that would not occur until hours after the clock time in which his body existed."

I tried not to react to this news. My mother studied me intensely, awaiting some sort of derisory comment of disbelief. But I kept steady and waited for her to finish.

She went on. "He could hear voices from the future. So, he used this knowledge in a way that he did not divulge to anyone but me. He would attend race meetings, meditate deeply and overhear which horse would win. His gambling was not really a gamble at all. He built up a massive fund for the Foundation from his betting activities. Just before he died, he told me the secret as he appointed me to be the Foundation President."

"So did you ever attempt to meditate like him and hear the future?"

"I tried but could not attain that level of engagement with alternative time perceptions."

"Well, I'm glad you've told me the truth about my father," I said. "And thank you for explaining about your work."

"Please do not tell others about Mohindra's legacy."

"I promise."

My mother walked slowly into the house as I sauntered off to the last bookmaker in the city who had not banned me.

BOOK FOUR

INTERLUDE

I was traveling back home. I had no intention of seeing the Tzadik again. In fact, I think I had decided that I would cease writing short stories altogether. Perhaps I could return to my former life as a violinist and composer. Imagine my surprise when, seated in a quiet corner of my local pub with a pint of excellent ale in my hand, I felt a tap on my shoulder. I turned and standing there was Sachs.

"Tell me." He began, "why did you not send me any stories?"

Uninvited, he sat down opposite me, expecting an answer.

"I am not sure you could have helped me," I replied.

"Of course not. It is the Tzadik who wants to read what his students write."

"So why did he say that you were going to give marks to us all?"

Sachs looked uncomfortable. Blushing, he said "I was as shocked as you when he announced that. I had no intention of scoring fellow students' stories. I think he was just being mischievous by suggesting it."

I thought for a moment. "Perhaps he wanted to see who would want to send their work to you. Did you get any responses?"

Sachs nodded. "Yes, just a couple: I passed them on to the Tzadik. I can let you see copies if you like."

And with that, he opened his briefcase and drew out these texts.

"I don't think you will like them: they are quite political. You can easily guess who wrote them. One was by the Chinese American woman: the other by her friend, the Kurdish student. I did not know their names. His was entitled 'friendship lost."

FRIENDSHIP LOST

Roj was my best friend, but not any longer. As a fellow Kurd, he is still my brother-in-arms, but I doubt that he will ever think of me as a brother again. While Roj remained in the countryside, I left as a young man and my path led me to working in cities overseeing the rental and sale of prestigious buildings.

Roj always knew his son, Masoud, was exceptional. It was not just the normal paternal pride in a gifted son who had easily defeated him in a game of chess when Masoud was only five years old. It was Masoud's unusual maturity demonstrated when he instantly went forward to help anyone he saw in distress.

But there was nothing the little boy could do as he ran to help his mother when she collapsed after walking up the mountain path to their home, carrying two buckets of water. Her heart failure left a gaping hole in their family. I got the villagers to club together to help Roj in the weeks after the death. Then, day by day, Roj slowly pulled together his life to make a home for himself and his son. Masoud seemed to spend every spare hour with the old chess board I had gifted him playing imaginary games against imaginary opponents whose defeat he dreamt would bring his mother back from the dark underworld into which she had fallen.

I told Roj about the annual Turkish chess tournament. "Why don't you let Masoud try his luck there?" Thinking it might help him get over the loss of his mum, Roj applied. They had to walk all the way to the city and Roj was under no illusion about his poor ability in the game. They made an unlikely couple of applicants, but Roj had to enter so that Masoud could take part as children were not allowed to enter unaccompanied.

I followed the tournament closely as I am a keen chess player although I play at nothing like the level required in the tournament. Diaco, one of the International Masters participating, was drawn against Masoud and, playing with white pieces, rapidly gained a strong position against the child. But, struggling as he might, all he could manage was a draw. "You are a very slippery player!" Diaco declared but Masoud was dissatisfied with his own performance. The next two games against much weaker opponents saw him win very quickly which, again, brought him up against Diaco who had won his intervening games.

On television I watched the confrontation. "We meet again," the smiling adult announced and, as a surprise, held out his hand to shake before the game began. As he extended his unexpected hand, he found that Masoud had already brought up his arm to meet Diaco's hand. It was as if Masoud had already predicted the unusual greeting.

The game followed a similar line as the first, but now with Masoud playing with the white pieces, it rapidly became obvious that the boy had a better grasp of how to play the middle game than Diaco had demonstrated. Despite furious resistance, Diaco resigned as the endgame dissolved into an easily winning position for Masoud.

The next round, when the winners of the early matches, played two games (one with white, one with black) against one another in a knockout phase found Masoud progressing in a way that attracted the attention of various commentators, always on the lookout for the next superstar. His demolition of the only Grand Master in the tournament had to wait until the final head-to-head. He beat the famous champion in both games, playing both white and black, and won the money prize that he had to give to Roj because Masoud was too young to have a bank account.

"How did you do it?" an American journalist asked. "Have you always played chess?"

Masoud frowned. "I'm not sure," he began. "It's as if I see the board as it looks in a few minutes time. I blink and I see the board now. Then it's obvious how to get from the here-and-now to the position I want a few minutes away." Diaco had watched the games and listened to this description. He recalled his surprise at finding Masoud's hand, already extended and waiting to shake his, even before he had decided to make this unusual gesture. "The boy can see the future," he told the journalist.

"What does he mean?" Roj asked his son. "No one can see the future." Masoud shrugged. "I don't know what he means. If I could have seen the future, I would have run down the hill and dragged up the water buckets so my mum would still be with us." Roj held his son's head in his arms as Masoud began to cry.

The organisng committee of the Rome Chess Tournament were inviting many of the world's finest players. With huge financial prizes on offer, no one turned down an invitation and several were cross at not being invited. But the committee was keen to invite not only the very top Grand Masters, but also a smattering of young up-and-coming talent. So, the decision to invite Masoud caused much ill feeling amongst high ranking, established players who were overlooked.

"It is a hell of a risk inviting the child," the Chairman admitted to the committee, but he is the only Kurd ever to have beaten such strong opposition. "And it will attract very good mass media coverage which is what our financial sponsors want."

"There is a problem," the committee secretary announced. "The child's father says he has not enough money to travel to Italy. The prize Masoud won in Turkey has been spent on his education, on food, on bare necessities in their mountain home. He won't be able to fly here."

The committee quickly agreed to pay for Masoud and Roj to attend the competition. Their arrival at the airport was greeted with film crews and Italian tv coverage that even made a little item at the end of the national news.

The noise and bustle surrounding the players entering the tournament venue disorientated Roj: but Masoud seemed to know exactly where to go and walked purposefully through the crowd of chess enthusiasts until he reached the Committee chairman who was talking into a microphone being held up by a BBC reporter from London.

"Excuse me," Masoud said in hesitant English, "but can you tell me where I play my games, please?" The chairman recognised the little player and broke off the tv interview to accompany him onto the platform. "Thank you," Masoud said and smiled at the man.

Roj was asked how his son knew English. "American television; he likes the old westerns." And, very quickly, Masoud's opponents learnt that he enjoyed playing like a gunslinger determined to outgun anyone who stood in his way. "He plays his moves almost instantly," one commentator remarked. "He never runs into any time trouble. It's almost as if he is rushing to get to a position he has already foreseen."

One of the strongest players in the world, a contender for the world championship, found himself running seriously low on time against Masoud. The position had developed into an unorthodox pattern where Masoud seemed to be leaving weak backward pawns that looked too inviting not to take. But the temptation required a lot of calculation before deciding whether it was worth the attack. The decision to grab the pawns was shown to be ill-conceived as Masoud's counterattack left his opponent open to a brilliant exchange of pieces and a mating net that featured in the next day's international coverage as 'the best candidate for the brilliancy prize'.

Roj told me that he wanted to protect his son from the media's over-enthusiastic approaches. Once the games for the day had finished, he ushered him away to their hotel room without giving the interviewers the chance to waylay Masoud. All the tv press got were shots of the little boy being hurried away by his dad, and commentary teams discussing what the games showed.

"It's almost uncanny," one former world champion said who was not taking part in the tournament. "Masoud plays so fast that it gives his opponent no chance to think tactically without using up their own time. He seems to enjoy complicating positions, so it is easy to make mistakes if you start running out of time. And he never runs out of time. One match, you'll see, he beat his opponent in sixteen moves and used just ten seconds! Unbelievable!!"

The Committee Chairman was basking in the glory of his controversial decision to invite Masoud. Those committee members who had doubted his strategy were convinced by the additional sponsorship deals already coming through – even if they understood nothing whatsoever about chess. Turkish television reported it as a triumph for their nation, as did Iraq. No one seemed to know exactly where this Kurdish family lived in terms of national boundaries. Roj was asked from which country he came. He said he had been given a Turkish passport although he did not speak Turkish. Iraqi television reported that Masoud's mother had been buried in Iraq. One BBC commentator decided to ask a linguist to discover what language Roj spoke. "It's Sorani," came the response, "like most Kurds living in Iraq."

"Which country do you come from?" was shouted at Masoud the next day as he arrived to play. "I am a Kurd," the little boy replied in English. That reply was not broadcast in either Iraq or Turkey. The battle to claim Masoud as their own had just begun.

With all the noise and attention surrounding the little boy, Masoud had not slept well the night before. In his first game in the morning, he complained he was tired and could not see the board very clearly. Roj was worried about his son's health and less about the chess board. Playing white, Masoud managed to squeeze an unlikely draw against another young player. He asked if he could have a rest, and the Chairman ruled that this was allowed under the rules of the tournament if he could complete two more games in the afternoon. In a back room, resting quietly on a plush settee, Masoud fell asleep and had to be woken for lunch. Roj asked if he felt well enough to continue and was astonished by Masoud's reply.

"I will win the first game in twenty moves, but the second will go to fifty before he resigns."

Assuming that this was just the bravado of the overconfident, young genius, Roj brought him to the platform after he had eaten. Masoud adopted his usual swashbuckling approach and stormed all over his opponent's position. He checkmated the astonished Grand Master who was playing black, without using more than sixty seconds on his own clock. The game took exactly twenty moves. The second game, against a world champion contender who was already the favourite to win the tournament, was an entirely different affair. The bearded Russian champion played a well analyzed set of moves that had been examined in depth by leading chess computers. It was clear that the champion was very familiar with the options and matched Masoud for time. Neither seemed to spend more than a couple of seconds on moving their pieces. It was on move forty-five that Masoud suddenly exclaimed in Sorani "that is a mistake!"

The Russian did not understand what the little boy had said and asked the referee to tell the boy not to speak during the game. Masoud understood what he had been told but turned to Roj and whispered "My opponent should not have made that move. Do you think I should let him retake it as he is going to lose quite easily now? Until now it has been quite interesting, but he has spoiled the game by making such a silly move."

"What is he saying?" Roj was asked. Roj reported his son's whisper word for word, and the translation provided across the television screens had watchers laughing and wondering what Masoud had seen that no one else had managed. Five moves later and all was revealed. The champion resigned, just as Masoud had predicted.

Masoud winning the Rome tournament made headlines. Chess was rarely the stuff of major news stories: but the little boy's apparent genius together with his modest background and pleasing, courteous treatment of others made him a model star for the voracious news editors on the lookout for a hero away from sordid politics. Roj did his best to protect his son from the media but, truth be told, Masoud seemed to handle questioners with an easy assurance that combined innocence with the extraordinary way that he always delivered instant responses. He never hesitated. It was as if he already had time to prepare his answer before the questioner had even started asking.

"I can hear their questions even before they open their mouths," he told Roj.

"How is that possible?"

"I have no idea. It's the same in chess. I can see the board as it will be laid out ages before we get to that part of the game."

"I don't understand."

"Nor do I. I've been able to jump between phases of time ever since I can remember."

Roj, ever mindful and suspicious of how his son might be viewed as a freak by those who did not know him, advised Masoud to say nothing about his 'phasing'. "If asked, just say you see how the pieces can move for you to win. Don't say anything about being able to see or hear into the future."

At school, term had begun and Masoud settled happily learning with his friends. They did not regard him as anything other than a gentle boy who sometimes got sad when he remembered he had lost his mum. They knew he was good at a game that most of them did not know how to play. One older boy, however, was aware of the young child's international status, and decided that it was time to show the little man who was the real boss at the school. The bully was determined to pick a fight with Masoud. To get the quiet chess genius to come out from amongst his friends, the big boy brought a long knife to school with the intention of threatening Masoud's little friends.

But before he could bring his plan into operation, Masoud rushed up to his teacher to report that his friend was being threatened by the bully. The teacher walked out to see what was happening, but there was nothing to see. But just as he turned to come back into the building, he saw the knife owner running out of the building towards Masoud's little friend. The bully was detained by the teacher and his knife confiscated.

"How did you know he was going to attack your friend with a knife?" he was asked. "I just saw it before he managed to start," was the puzzling reply.

What was still more puzzling was the accusation made against Masoud that he was cheating at exams. There was no way that he had access to the examination room and the exam papers were only distributed from the sealed envelope a few moments before being placed face-down on the desks. But even before the students were told to turn over the exam questions, Masoud raised his hand to ask the exam invigilator why the wrong exam papers had been passed out.

"How do you know they are not the right ones? You've not even seen them yet."

"I can read that they are the ones for tomorrow."

Sure enough, when the documents for that day and the next were read by the invigilators, Masoud's statement was found to be correct. The envelopes had been incorrectly labelled.

Roj was called into the school to answer embarrassing questions about how his son had accessed the examination papers even before the school had had the opportunity to open the envelopes. He just shrugged his shoulders and reminded them that his son appeared to have extraordinary powers, demonstrated in the toughest intellectual world of international chess tournaments, that no one – including his father – could understand. "So perhaps when he says he can read future layouts, that might include printed instructions. All I can say is that he himself does not understand it. But I know that he would never cheat as he can pass exams without recourse to cheating. You know how intelligent he is."

The school had no alternative but to accept Roj's statement. But the head teacher decided to alert the relevant government authorities that Masoud might have abilities which might be of service if used by the State. He wrote: 'Masoud averted a knife attack before it was launched, and this year he has read exam papers before they have even been opened. The accusation that his chess brilliance is based upon an uncanny ability to see the future may be of great interest to those in government concerned with the safety and security of the public.'

Masoud's profession was already being carved out in a future that even he had not foreseen.

Roj told me about their visitors from Ankara. The two men wore very smart suits and asked to speak with Roj before meeting Masoud. But Masoud walked in before they started to say anything to his father and explained that his powers for seeing the future could only be used for people's benefit. He wanted nothing to do with criminal activity or reporting things that might hurt those being observed through what he called "phased time".

"How do you know what we are going to talk to your father about?"

"I have already heard what you are going to say."

And, as if impelled by forces that they were unable to resist, the men then made their prepared speech to Roj ("word for word as I have already heard it", according to Masoud).

Roj told me that he was suspicious but prepared to hear the men out. And, as the day wore on, he became less anxious about how they wanted to deploy his son. "We just want him to forewarn us of any danger that could threaten innocent lives."

Masoud was just a teenaged chess superstar with an uncanny and inexplicable facility that he was keen to avoid being abused by people with evil intentions. But he was an innocent in the ways of the world of international politics. Roj had always been a fine example of a hardworking Kurd who would always help his fellow strugglers. Unlike me, he had never joined any political parties or movements. But he felt sure that the men from Ankara would never want to have any harm come to Masoud. They even called his son "our greatest asset" – which did not sound like a title you would give to someone you would then put into any danger.

Masoud dropped out of chess competitions in the coming year or two as he was paid to attend intensive training in Ankara that prepared him for exposure to hearing and reading what some men wanted to inflict upon others. He was willing and able to report what was being planned to his handlers who were delighted by the unique information he provided. As a result, several carefully prepared and secret attacks against sensitive areas of the Turkish State that would otherwise have been ill-defended were foiled, and the perpetrators captured before they could carry out their plans. "You have been vital in preventing serious injury and deaths in our country," he was told. "But you must continue to keep your part in these operations secret as we do not want you to become a target."

When Roj took me into his confidence to tell me about this potential threat against Masoud, he wanted to know if there was anything he or I could do to ensure his son's safety. The men from Ankara were keeping their distance as they told Masoud that their presence as his protectors would imply that he should become a target. "It is better if you just continue your career as a leading chess player and say nothing about the work you do with us in the capital."

The Interzonal Chess tournament featured far more blitz games than classical: so, players were required to move very quickly without much chance to calculate positions. This suited Masoud down to the ground and his rapid progress through the early stages again attracted considerable attention from both keen followers of the game as well as the sensation-loving sections of the popular press. It was while he was heavily engaged in winning the tournament that I approached our leader with a plan to disturb the Turkish oppressors of our Kurdish people. I wrote nothing down but explained in some detail how the action should be carried out. The false documents were all drawn up before the tournament was over and Masoud again went to Ankara.

Unaware of my trickery, Masoud faithfully reported what he read remotely as an apparent plan by our Kurdish freedom fighters. He read we were acting as part of a coordinated plan to seize high-profile people and call for recognition of our nation before releasing them. Through my work, I had an intimate knowledge of the status and usage being made of several important buildings in the capital. Our bogus documents purported to show that a few were being used as launching-off points by Kurdish militants in a coordinated assault upon key targets. The buildings were described as being disguised as official offices of foreign States (which, in fact, they were!).

The day marked for the assault began when Turkish Special Forces stormed the unsuspecting staff at each of the buildings, taking many prisoners although puzzled by the absence of any obvious Kurds amongst those taken. The embassies of the countries that had been renting the offices for their staff demanded to know why they had been targeted. The embarrassment caused by the violence used against innocent staff working for the Russian, American and Chinese ambassadors was a significant victory for our people without putting any of us in danger. The sole focus of Ankara's anger was directed at Masoud who was suspected of deliberately misleading his handlers for the cause of the Kurds. But his previously unblemished track record and his celebrity status as one of the world's greatest chess players made it impossible for them to take official action against him.

However, one of the handlers – a maverick operator in his own right – decided that he was going to take some "unofficial action" against the young man. Masoud was hit on the head with a truncheon and was in hospital for a month. When he emerged, it was without his God-given ability to "phase", without the fearsome capacity to win chess games at the highest standard, and whose father, Roj, now no longer talks to me."

I was unsure how to respond to this story. I said to Sachs: "Do you think this is a total invention or do you suspect it contains some elements of truth?" Sachs shrugged but said that he was pretty sure that the other story reflected the elderly Chinese American woman's personal experience. He said: "although she obviously knows her Greek myths, to me it feels as if it's based on a very troubling reminiscence."

THE TEIRESIAS DILEMMA

I feel old now and have seen some terrible things. I do not see very much now as my sight has started to fail. Perhaps it is better that I cannot see what will happen for, if it mimics the past, I would prefer to know nothing of the future.

There are certain critical moments in your life around which everything else pivots. If you are a reader with a sensitive disposition, maybe you should stop now. Many of those moments have been terrible for me but that does not include the moment I met Don.

My parents had fled China before I was born. Their little grocery store in a Californian town was near a wealthy winery. Don was the eldest son of the Caster winery owners and came to pick up supplies every week. The first time he and I met landed us both on our backs! He was walking in just as I was walking out; neither of us was looking where we were going. He leapt up to ensure that I was not hurt whilst I was apologising for knocking him down. We joked about the first impression we had made upon each other for many years afterwards.

I do not think that either of our parents approved of our marriage. The Casters felt that Don could have found a higher-class wife. My traditionalist parents obviously felt that my life should have been devoted to a suitable

Chinese husband. Inter-racial marriage in 1930s America was not common but we were young, reckless, and really did not care what our parents thought. Although Don's parents reluctantly gave their blessing when they saw how happy we both were, his younger brother, Rex, remained distant from the outset.

The economic depression affected us all. My parent's store was losing money so badly that they decided it was time for them to return to China. I cried as we saw them off on a steamship out of San Francisco: but I could not count that as a truly terrible moment. No! Terrible moments are events from which you never really recover. My parent's departure was just a temporary dislocation in the flow of our lives: a disruption whose ripples were soon erased by greater events.

The Depression even gave cash flow problems to the Caster Winery. I think many of our friends assumed that Don would be looking to the Winery for his career. However, even without the financial problems that clearly troubled his parents, Don never wanted to be reliant on the family business. His decision to join the army gave him independence and saw us move around to many army camps. And it was in a dusty barracks hospital in Nevada where our daughter, Jo, was born in 1940. She was a sweet child and Don adored her.

When the Japanese attacked Pearl Harbour, Don's was one of the first units to be brought into active service in the Pacific. I still shake when I recall the first terrible moment in my life when the telegram arrived informing me that Don had been killed. His body was brought back and buried in the family plot beside the winery. I held little Jo, asleep in my arms, whilst the Minister read the service over his grave. Four servicemen lifted their rifles and fired a volley, waking Jo up with a start as if she knew that she would never see her loving father again. Don's parents insisted that Jo, their sole grandchild, and her mother live with them and their other son, Rex. As I had nowhere else to go, I accepted their offer.

Now here is a strange thing. My name on my birth certificate is Soo Li. My parents wrote it as 蘇李. Yet Don's parents always spelt my name Sue Lee. It was as if they could never accept my Chinese lineage. Of course, you could say, "What is in a name?" I am the same person no matter who spells or misspells my name. Yet I feel the way that you are seen is affected by the name that others call you. I look Chinese and so does Jo – a fact that never seemed to cause any problem to Don. But for his parents and for Rex, it was always an issue simmering away underneath everything we did.

Whilst living in the Winery, I tried to be as helpful as possible. I learnt many of the techniques used by the key staff and could easily have become more active if permitted by the Casters. But they seemed to feel that I was somehow trespassing on sacred ground when trying to participate in the most critical stages of the winemaking process. Rex, in particular, made it clear that although I may have been Don's wife and that I was officially Soo Caster, my name gave me no rights over the Winery. He was moody most of the time; a temperament that I believe was his from birth. His parents, however, constantly excused him for his bad attitude because of the loss of his brother. But whenever I showed any signs of depression, they regarded this as the effect of "Chinese blood". The loss of my husband and the father of my child, apparently, should not have made any impression on my "simple, oriental mind."

The war ended before Rex could be called up: a matter of intense relief to his parents although I must admit that I would not have been sorry to see him depart. His presence cast a gloom over the household from which I wanted to shield Jo. I wanted her to enjoy a happy childhood, despite the lack of a father. And perhaps she did enjoy the comparative freedom to roam about the Sonoma Valley vineyards whereas other children of her age were confined to the backyards of San Francisco suburbs. Her innocence was not to continue for long. First, the revolution in the Chinese homeland impacted indirectly upon us. My parents wrote to tell us that they had fled their ancestral home and gone to live in faraway Shanghai. Their unhappiness seemed to seep across the Pacific and my natural reaction, to want to rush to their side to help them through their latest crisis, probably cast yet another shadow across Jo's horizon. But far worse was to follow.

The Korean War at last drew Rex away from the Winery: but not for long. He was flown home after being shot in the thigh. His recovery left him with a lifelong limp. His anger at being injured seemed only to be assuaged by heavy use of alcohol. His mood was so dreadful that he would swear at his over-protective parents and even attempt to hit me when he was drunk. Then, one appalling day whilst I was in town shopping, Jo – now aged thirteen – came across Rex in a particularly black mood. Her tears that greeted me when I returned home were accompanied by a graphic description of how her uncle had raped her. I burst into Rex's room to confront him: maybe even to tear out his eyes! But he was not there and my report to his parents was met with total disbelief and denial. Eventually Rex returned, sick with drink, only to tell his parents that Jo was obviously inventing the story and that it was probably at my instigation that she had concocted such a tale. Despite all the evidence to the contrary, the parents regarded Jo as a treacherous liar and stood by their last-surviving son.

The next day I packed all our belongings and left the Caster Winery forever. Jo, still crying and in pain, fled with me vowing to gain revenge on her uncle. But we were powerless in the face of the Caster's prominence in the community. The local police believed the parental assertion that their son was with them far from the Winery when the alleged assault took place. The police interviewed Jo asking her who the stranger who attacked her might have been as it could not have been Rex. Jo, now living with me in a tiny apartment in San Francisco's Chinatown, could not understand the question as she knew who Rex was. The investigation went nowhere, and we lost contact with the Casters as I had to spend time working in a nearby restaurant to pay the rent and feed myself and my daughter. It was only after working for a couple of months that we realised that Jo was pregnant.

Our elderly Chinese neighbours helped us through the difficulties of the coming months. When I was at work, Jo could weep in their parlour and always found a ready ear to hear her despair. They told me I should not take it to heart that Jo blamed me for not protecting her, for not being at the Winery when her uncle attacked her, for not being strong enough to force the Casters to admit the truth. Even after Jo's son was born, she still regarded me with a mixture of anger and contempt. Maybe this period was really the worst moment of my life – a moment that was somehow prolonged for three years. Jo could not accept that Edward was really her son: he was more like an intruder who somehow had gained access to her broken family. By the time she was sixteen, she could no longer stand being in the same apartment as her mother and her son. Jo left us and the community treated Eddy as if he were my baby.

Where did Jo go? You would think that I should have known. After all, I was a good mother who should have been looking out for her teenaged daughter. But she had rejected me so profoundly that she wanted nothing more to do with her mother – nor her son. She cut herself off from us and my enquiries only discovered that she was living in some sort of commune in Haight Ashbury. Now I know that by the time that the sixties arrived, she was a mainstream hippie … but I am jumping ahead. There was much to happen to us before that.

Eddy was a strangely quiet baby. He seemed curious about what happened around him; but made very little sound as he observed the adults circling about him. I believed that he may have been deaf; but he responded well to hearing tests. I worried that he had some mental defect that was preventing the development of language skills. But I should not have been anxious. Quite suddenly, just after his third birthday, Eddy suddenly spoke as if he had always known both Chinese and English. He spoke like a little adult. It was a shock, and neighbours would come to listen to the little man babbling in both languages. But, despite the generosity of our neighbours and the presence of my daughter in a nearby suburb, there was a greater call on me that drew me back to China. My parents were now both quite unwell and elderly. There was no one to care for them and I felt that it was my duty to be by their side in the final years of their lives. Leaving messages for Jo that she probably ignored, Eddy and I departed for Shanghai in 1960.

I can recall sailing across the Pacific as if it were yesterday. Yet I cannot remember our arrival. It is peculiar how the memory plays tricks like that. Eddy was a little angel as the ship tossed about whilst I felt nauseous for hours on end. I think my parents must have met us and spirited me off to bed. It took days for the effects of the journey to wear off. By the time I had recovered, Eddy and his great grandparents were firm friends. Of course, he did not know that they were great grandparents as he always believed (and I hope still believes) that I am his mother. His upbringing was truly shared between myself and my parents. Their love and understanding were as remarkable as their poverty in the slums of Shanghai. Sharing the tenement landing with us was Pauli Pousse, a French journalist. He and my father would wile away the time playing chess and discussing politics. Over the coming months I pieced together how Pauli had come to be living in such an uninviting environment.

Pauli had begun his life writing wine reviews for a local newspaper in southwest France. He described his career as "falling upwards" until he became a foreign correspondent for a well-known left-wing journal. He was posted to Vietnam in 1953 to cover the war in which his countrymen were unceremoniously despatched from the country. Pauli's reports were published by the journal; but he and the journal were reviled as traitors by politicians on all sides. His 'letters from Vietnam' revealed the poverty of French colonial thinking and the advisability of leaving the Vietnamese to govern their own nation. The journal lost its readership, Pauli lost his job, but the newly established Communist government of China welcomed him as a hero who had "told the truth in a sea of lies". He was given a home in Shanghai and invited to write propaganda articles that could be distributed to the western press. As the years wore on, he tired of writing such pap. His articles became increasingly hackneyed and less focused on a hatred for "the enemies of Chairman Mao". By the time that I arrived in China, Pauli had lost his political position, lost his influence with those in power, and lost his desirable accommodation to one of the rising stars in the local Party.

As America became increasingly involved in Vietnam, Pauli regained a little of his lost status. His articles were published in Europe again and the Chinese establishment respected his knowledge of the western media – although not enough to provide him with any more salubrious accommodation. But he did not seem to mind as he was becoming a near-permanent visitor to our flat. It took me some time to realise that, although he and my father were firm friends, his attachment to our family was becoming focused upon me. His attentions were so courteously hidden that my mother had to tell me that to everyone else it was obvious that he liked me. Perhaps it was his kindness to Eddy that most appealed to me at the outset. As an awkward teenager, Eddy needed a trustworthy father figure. Pauli, a classical scholar with a cultured outlook and amusingly tortured Chinese, provided Eddy with both a man to look up to and an unending source of humour. I was genuinely pleased when this good and honourable man asked my parents for permission to seek my hand in marriage. It was he who launched me into my later career as an author, writing about the influence of Greek and Roman myths on life today.

I am looking at Pauli now as I write this account. He is asleep on the couch and remains the only human being with whom I feel I can share all my secret fears and ambitions. It was he who foresaw what was about to happen in China. It was he who advised his new son, Eddy, to join the Revolutionary Guard. He explained to me that this would ensure our son's survival in a time of chaos, madness, and murder. But the so-called Cultural Revolution could not save my parents. Hundreds of us were taken in trucks out to the barren countryside where we were expected to undertake "honest work" for the revolution rather than enjoy the "decadent lifestyle" of westernised urban society. Pauli and I survived despite being subjected to two years of tilling poor soil: but my parents perished in the first year and I did not discover this until we eventually were allowed to return to Shanghai. They had been taken to another part of our wonderful country in the north: and the cold had been too much for them. They were buried beside one another, and I have visited their grave in the years since.

But my contempt for the "revolutionary" movement that swept them there can never be assuaged.

I do not want to write about what Pauli and I went through. It is a period that my mind has attempted to block out of memory. Re-telling the experience would cause me nothing but pain. This was another "terrible moment" that was prolonged for twenty-four horrible months. Instead, I want to tell you what happened to Eddy. Commander Ong has recounted to me more than once how impressed he was by "your remarkable son". It was this same commander who arranged for Pauli and me to be transferred back to Shanghai after being petitioned by Eddy. What so impressed this man about my teenaged grandson? It was not his dedication to the Revolution: Eddy hated to talk about politics. It was not his love of the country: it was never clear to which country Eddy felt he belonged. It was the talent that he demonstrated as a marksman. "I have never seen a cadet make a one hundred percent score in the first three visits to the rifle range."

So, Eddy was rapidly "promoted" into the élite core of snipers. And, as irony would have it, he was smuggled into Pauli's old haunt in Saigon as part of the supposedly secret support provided by the Chinese army to the Vietcong resistance to the American invasion. Eddy Pousse presented himself as a friendly, English-speaking, pro-American youngster keen to work for his American friends. Officially he worked as a bartender in the city centre. Unofficially, he identified senior officers to whom he served drinks before assassinating them. Commander Ong told me that Eddy's Kalashnikov rifle was hidden on the roof inside the chimney. He would creep up and pick off his target before returning innocently behind the bar. The bar owner was in league with Eddy and covered for him whilst he undertook his deadly work. It was at the crossroads one block up from his rooftop perch where Eddy shot and killed one of his regular drinkers. The officer who walked with a pronounced limp was Colonel Rex Caster.

To Commander Ong, the shot was fired by a soldier obeying orders. To Pauli, it was fired by a liberator helping rid Vietnam of a foreign invader. To Eddy – who knew nothing of the relationship he shared with his target – he was an unwitting instrument within a wider scheme of things in which old men die at the hands of the young. To me, it was the execution of a rapist.

Commander Ong was an unusual man. Outwardly he was the epitome of the revolutionary who had dedicated himself to the People's Liberation Army. But outward appearances in China can be deceiving. His father had been a wayward, Catholic priest. His mother, attracted by the cassocked Frenchman, had conceived her son in the church vestry one Sunday after Mass. Both parents cared for their son, and he had been brought up bi-lingual. So, Pauli and he became firm friends, speaking French (Pauli's Chinese has always been quite idiosyncratic). And I am convinced that it was this that led to the Commander's idea to have Eddy penetrate further into the American military machine.

Pauli wrote a note to Commander Ong – a play on words: "Eddy pousse l'americain de Vietnam". I read this as 'Eddy is pushing the American presence from Vietnam'. But the Commander read it as 'Eddy Pousse, the Vietnamese American' and it gave him the idea that our boy could pose as an American, with his Californian accent, and perhaps infiltrate into their command structure. He issued his orders accordingly and, like a cork tossed along a raging river, Eddy plunged in with conviction. Within months Eddy was on a ship bound for the United States. He was classified as a friendly foreigner, in jeopardy from the advancing North Vietnamese enemy. Eddy confused the immigration officers in San Francisco by posing as a returning American whose papers had been destroyed during a fire fight in Saigon. Commander Ong was delighted by his protégé's improvisatory skills but what he failed to recognise was Eddy's lack of firm adherence to any ideology. Eddy Pousse was being swept along on a life torrent where his personal room for manoeuvre was severely limited.

Pauli smiled at the news that Eddy had joined in the final anti-war rallies being held in Berkeley. "Perhaps he should not admit to being a war veteran," Pauli said to Ong one evening. Ong frowned as he could not see what advantage could be gained by Eddy putting his time into the anti-war movement. "How can he gain a senior military position by protesting against the war?" But, of course, Eddy was no longer being guided by his distant master. Proximity to other forces was drawing him to a seemingly inevitable meeting.

Eddy did not wait to discuss his wedding plans with me. He just rushed into the affair with a fellow anti-war campaigner. She was older than him and led the life of a waif and stray around the bay area. He had no reason to believe that he, Eddy Pousse, was related in any way to Jo Caster. The news of their wedding was another of my "terrible moments". I was transfixed by the words as they appeared in a letter from Eddy to Pauli and me. If that were not enough, the letter contained yet another "little surprise" (Pauli's description). Rex Caster's death without an apparent heir had led to a search for his nearest surviving relative. No one thought of trying to track me down, the widow of Don Caster. Instead, Jo had been traced and was informed soon after her marriage that she had inherited the Caster winery. Eddy wrote to tell Pauli and I that he and his bride had now moved into the estate, and both were very happy "although we would certainly benefit from Pauli's expertise in wine as neither Jo nor I know much about it." Pauli finished reading the letter to me and I shielded my eyes which, although losing their sight, seemed to see far more than they wanted.

My dilemma has been complicated by the fact that the great winery will almost certainly fall into decline without the knowledge that Pauli and I could bring to the business. It is unlikely that Jo will discover that Eddy shot her abuser as he will probably stay silent about his part in the war. Even if he did reveal himself to her, this may not damage their relationship. But, of course, my appearance at the estate would instantly bring about a catastrophic crisis in the marriage of the two new owners.

Jo knows nothing of my relationship to Eddy. Her long-lost son was a baby named Edward Li. Now she is married to a French-speaking, Chinese-speaking American named Eddy Pousse. Provided that she does not discover his other names, she may stay blithely happy in her newfound, and much-deserved, wealth with a young lover who apparently shares her hatred for war and is prepared to demonstrate it.

My vision may be failing but I feel that my "terrible moments" are being relived for me in plain sight. And now I seem to see far more than the young people in America can see but I wish I did not. My dilemma is whether to remain silent and hide in Shanghai or whether to return to California and reveal all our true names. "But what is in a name?" Pauli asks. Commander Ong says he feels as if he has lost a son. Jo has inadvertently gained one. Perhaps I should just give mine up.

I handed the script back to Sachs.
I said, "I wonder what our Tzadik thought of that."
"I've no idea. He has not been in touch since our last class. But I found the entire tale quite troubling."
"Perhaps we'll hear from him soon."
Sachs nodded and rose to leave and said, "I hope we meet again if he calls us together."
I nodded politely and went back to my pint of ale.

BOOK FIVE

GREEK HOLIDAY

Although I was quite tired after all the travelling, the winter was drawing in and I did not fancy months of rain, snow and low temperatures. I decided to splash out and spend a few months in the eastern Mediterranean – far away from the chill winds of the Atlantic. I hoped that I might enjoy some relaxing time in a warm sun. Perhaps I could write stories inspired by these surroundings.

THE PITHOS

It is September when insects become drowsy. My son was poking around a wasp nest and only stopped after I told him this story.

"Listen as I tell you how Zeus punished mankind after the Titan Prometheus stole the secret of fire from the gods. In retribution he created Pandora to become the wife of Prometheus's brother, Epimetheus. Ignoring Prometheus's warnings, Epimetheus brought Pandora home together with the wedding gift provided by Zeus. The gift was a storage jar containing all the evils and the virtues of this world which escaped when Pandora innocently opened it.

The jar (in Greek, 'pithos') was much later renamed a 'box' by Erasmus – presumably because it was easier to imagine the lid of a box being opened then shut quickly which would have permitted just one virtue, hope, to remain. Perhaps, since the acquisition of 'sfika' (Σφήκα translated as 'wasp' from the Greek), all we have left in this world is hope."

"Now, my son, the knowledge that we have of killing fellow human beings has reached extraordinary depths during modern warfare. But it was not until the creation of a sfika that a terrifying glimpse of the future was revealed – if only we had not ignored the warnings. The first sfika was created in Greece using a 3-d printer. Powered by a miniscule and dirt cheap 'motor', it flew with tiny 'wings' that made it look just like a wasp. The first developers saw it as a possible observation vehicle – like a very small drone. But, just as drones became used as weapons, the sfika began its inevitable ascent (or descent) into becoming the ultimate instrument of war.

It may have looked like a wasp, but the sfika had the capacity to carry very basic artificial intelligence capacity in its observation eye. The first use in a battle was almost useless. It flew towards enemy lines carrying a small explosive charge, eyeing its target remorselessly. But as it moved quite slowly, a soldier could bat it away as if playing baseball. The sfika would explode harmlessly nowhere near its target. If only we had given up on its development at that stage, we would not be where we are now.

The next two developments catapulted the sfika into becoming what we now recognise as the ultimate killing machine. Artificial intelligence capacity combined with access to 3-d printing gave strategists the idea that the sfika could reproduce itself. By producing hundreds, or thousands, of these 'wasps', it became almost impossible for soldiers to destroy them all before detonation. And so, their use on the frontline became normal. Again, if only we had stopped there, we may have been satisfied with our innovative skills. But the second development utilised the sfika 'brain' by programming the picture and profile of the individual commander of opposing troops. The sfika horde set out with just one target. When he was spotted, they swarmed over him, killing him with the combination of tiny explosives.

We are uncertain which nation decided to use the easily produced sfikas for assassination. Instead of explosives, a tiny 'wasp sting' of cyanide was carried and soon, the deaths of leading politicians, controversial celebrities (and even random individuals killed through sfika flight failures) made sfika production illegal in most countries. That made almost no difference as every country decided to maintain sfika capacity as a deterrent threat to the leader of any country intending to attack them.

It has been some years now since any nation has gone to war with another. Land disputes cannot be settled by military means without the almost inevitable death of the leaders of both nations. The acquisition of sfikas by organised crime syndicates was a major concern until opposition syndicates (as well as 'unofficial' police units) started using them. Some say we are now in the "happy" position of mutual deterrence ensuring peaceful coexistence. Others regard our existence as precarious and, like Epimetheus, find that there is just one thing remaining in the pithos – and that is hope.

In my garden this morning, poking around that wasp nest, my only hope is that you've not been stung by a random roaming sfika."

SIRENS

It is not true that our parents were gods. The notion that Achelous was our father and Terpsichore was our mother is ridiculous. And as for the vile slander that our music is designed to tempt passing sailors to their death: I think we can put that down to Calypso's enmity.

All three of us grew up in Sorrento and became leading singers in the court. Our training was undertaken by fine music teachers from Rome. The unwanted attention that was drawn to us by visiting nobility and religious leaders who seemed to believe that their status provided them with permission to make sexual advances led to our deciding to quit the mainland and set up home in the nearby island of Gallo Lungo. Here we believed we could complete our musical development and provide concert performances on the mainland from which to draw a reasonable income.

One of the posters survives: here is an English translation:

COME AND HEAR THE ANGELS SING

Peisinoe, Aglaope, and Thelxiepeia perform magical music whose perfection has drawn listeners from as far afield as Greece, Gaul, Spain and Britannia.

A collection where you can demonstrate your appreciation will be held halfway through and at the end of the concert. Please give generously.

Unfortunately, the concerts only attracted local listeners whose donations were decidedly ungenerous. Our income was hardly enough for us to survive. In desperation, we decided to try a new approach: invitations to international celebrities to attend a gala recital on the island itself. We advertised the events to be so select that only the very wealthy could afford to attend. This was a deliberate policy: we wanted to make the experience so special that we would callously turn away anyone whom we believed could not afford the exorbitant prices that we charged ticket holders even before they stepped onto the ferry bringing them to the island. This gave the trip a tinge of extravagance for which our potential listeners would be prepared to fork out far more than we ever charged when performing on the mainland. Ironically, we knew that exactly the same music was being performed as we had sung and played before in Sorrento.

When Ulysses ran aground on the island, it coincided on the day we were to welcome our paying guests. He was full of apologies for the intrusion, and we were thrown into a quandary as to how we should deal with him and his crew. We had no boat big enough to sail them back to the mainland. Aglaope had the best idea when it became obvious that we could not just evict them.

"They are just sailors who certainly could not pay for attending our concert," she said. "But we must retain the exclusive image of what we have to offer. We cannot have anyone who crashes here come to our concerts. I suggest that we stick them in the old outhouse, far away from our performance space."

Peisinoe added that perhaps we should insist that they place mufflers over their ears so that they could not hear the sounds at all. I thought beeswax could be used.

"That's a crazy idea, Thelxiepeia," they both said. But the sailors preferred this to sticking hot, woollen helmets over their heads as the evening temperatures were high and they did not want to suffer any unnecessary discomfort.

In the event, Ulysses slipped into the concert whilst his men were in the outhouse. We did not see him at the back of the hall. When the performance was over and the audience members started walking away, Ulysses was recognised by a visiting beauty – a fabled musician from an aristocratic family that had paid for her to attend. She offered Ulysses the use of her boat as his was so badly damaged. But she insisted that he return the boat to her island whilst awaiting his boat to be repaired. Despite his marriage to Penelope, he obviously saw no problem in moving in with Calypso which is how he got stuck with her. We now know she paid saboteurs to prevent the repair to the damaged boat.

All this had nothing to do with us. But Calypso told gullible chroniclers that we were "sirens" who had seduced Ulysses and his men. She elaborated her tale with disgusting suggestions that we murdered sailors after they had heard our singing. In fact, we made the abandoned crew feel at home as it was not their fault their leader had gone off with Calypso. We discovered that some of them had very fine singing voices, so we began arranging music with bass and tenor parts so that we could perform music for full choir. When Ulysses eventually escaped from Calypso's claws, he had to engage a new crew as most of them remained with us.

Some years later, we heard that Calypso had not only invented terrible tales about us as murderers but had also venomously cast aspersions upon our musical achievements. Instead of recognisng how we had evolved as a full choir by training our new male members up to a high standard, she pretended that we had been visited by a truly rough band, Jason and his argonauts. She put it about that this lot had challenged us to a singing competition and humiliated us by performing as if Orpheus himself was their leader. We suspect that her bile was raised because Ulysses had, finally, left her and she saw us and his old crew as somehow the cause of his rejection.

So, my faithful readers, please take care. Whatever you read, remember everything – absolutely everything – is written with some motive.

DROWNED

Phlebas the Phoenician, a fortnight dead,
Forgot the cry of gulls, and the deep sea swell
And the profit and loss.
*   A current under sea*
Picked his bones in whispers. As he rose and fell
He passed the stages of his age and youth
Entering the whirlpool.
*   Gentile or Jew*
O you who turn the wheel and look to windward,
Consider Phlebas, who was once handsome and tall
as you.

T.S. ELIOT
The Waste Land: Death by Water

Sailing from Tyre to Kition was a journey that his family never wanted to repeat. But Phlebas had been inspired by the other merchants who had begun colonisng the coastal strip of Cyprus. Some had made significant profits by working with the locals in extracting copper from shallow mines and selling it, at a high price, to the Egyptian and Greek traders who visited Tyre regularly. Personally, he preferred dealing with the local Jewish craftsmen who served anyone in Canaan. He did not like the way that the Egyptians would only sell to fellow Egyptians.

"But what have you got against the Greeks?" his wife's father asked.

"Nothing really. I'm just suspicious of what they do with the copper."

"You mean they might be making weapons."

"I suppose so."

"And you don't suspect that Jews would ever forge swords and helmets?"

"I don't know. But they always pay a fair price and don't appear very warlike."

"Oh! So, you think the Greeks are aggressive and hostile?"

"Well, uncle, I know that Alexander with whom you've traded has amassed his own private army. None of the Jews are like that: they seem more intent upon creating ornaments and decorations for their temple."

His uncle had tried dissuading him by pressuring his daughter not to sail the family across to Kition. And, truth be told, by the time they arrived both he and his wife were thinking that perhaps they should have done as he said and remained in Tyre. The boat appeared to be in good shape as it left, but it began showing its age soon after when the little hole in the hull created a leak that grew bigger as the journey progressed. By the time that Kition was sighted, all the passengers and crew were busy scooping water off the deck and emptying it over the side.

Miriam, his Jewish wife, feared that the boat would sink and her tall, handsome husband together with their musically gifted daughter would drown. Somehow, it never occurred to her that she might also perish. In her imagination, she was always the onlooker who stood aside from the action, a permanent reporter on what others were doing. So, as the boat limped into port, she was the last passenger to disembark as she helped everyone else onto the quay.

The captain thanked her for helping and said that he still had passengers who had booked their passage back to Tyre. His priority was to repair the ship's hull and set sail the day after. He needed help and would pay in cash. He wanted men who were not afraid to load heavy timbers onto the deck despite the ship listing heavily, weighed down by the water it was still carrying in the hold. Miriam volunteered her husband because she knew that they needed some ready cash.

Next day, with her daughter singing for tips in the local bar and her husband working for easy money at the dock, Miriam set out to find the shack that she knew had been set aside for them by Abraham, one of her relatives. He said he would charge them nothing at all as he never used the old hut he had once bought just to store goods ready for shipping.

The shack was easy to find and, despite Abraham's description, was not in bad shape. All it needed was some rudimentary repairs to the roof and floor covering to become quite habitable. With help from their neighbour, the roof was quickly patched up and straw to cover the floor was freely available in piles at the end of the street. She set out to collect her daughter before walking down to the pier where the boat was docked. The captain greeted them and asked them if her husband was going to return to work. She was puzzled and said that she had not seen him and had assumed he had been working on the boat.

"The last I saw of him," the captain said, "he said he was going to carry the heavy wooden cross planks from the store down to the dock for us to fit. But we never got the planks because he did not reappear."

It was two weeks before Miriam discovered her husband's body. It was badly decomposed. He was floating, face up, beside the pier. Birds had eaten his eyes, and their distraught daughter no longer recognised him. Despite his Phoenician background, his funeral featured the Kaddish so that as he and Miriam parted, they could go their separate ways.

THE ISLAND RAPE

1.ANN'S STORY

The island is full of flowers. The nuns used to tend them as if it were a penance. They would come back, sweaty and breathing hard, to tell the reverend Mother of their toils in the garden. And she would nod and bless them so they could feel forgiven for whatever sins they imagined they had committed. The girls in my dormitory would pretend to be peasants, kneel before me and bring offerings. "Oh! Sacred Ann! If we give you this bouquet, would you let us join you in Heaven?" And I would graciously accept the gift and say I might consider it. And we would giggle.

The convent garden had neat rows of flowers and vegetables. But the rest of the island is covered with a kaleidoscope of colour as the daisies, poppies, marigolds, lilies and roses compete with the broom thistles and coarse scrub for breathing space. Families carefully arrange bushes and flower beds before the front door of their homes; and the more affluent employ gardeners to crop creepers brightening the house walls. Peter's home has always presented a wonderful display that could be seen from the road as we walked to school.

Peter's family moved onto the island before I was born. His father bought the mansion from a Greek landowner who wanted to return to the mainland. His mother was kindly and would encourage me to make floral displays for the house. Even as a child, I would come into their garden and was allowed to pick flowers for her home. I was genuinely upset when she and her husband died in the car crash. I did not really know Peter's father: but I felt a strong attachment to his mother.

The convent sisters told us to pray for the souls of the crash victims, but most of the girls did not treat their social superiors with proper respect. As the parents were English, there was a strong feeling that they were foreign visitors whose real home was not on the island. The mansion and its gardens, however, were real enough and Peter's forced return from the English public school saw him making a life for himself here. His Greek was poor, and his fair skin made work under the sun painful. But his family's wealth allowed him to employ labourers to tend the crops. "You are managerial class," I would say to him. "You should not need to break your back on the land."

I think that Peter only really noticed me after his parents died. Before that his life was almost entirely spent in England. During the summer holiday, his parents would leave the island and visit faraway places with him: so, I only ever caught sight of him if he came home for Christmas. His athletic build and shock of fair hair attracted my attention whilst I was still with the sisters; but I dared not confide in them how I felt. The other girls would tell me which Greek youth they each fancied as the village boys found daily excuses to display their tanned bodies in the school playground. But I kept quiet as I knew early on that I was destined to marry better than that. So, whilst they flirted, I virtuously improved myself by learning the arts of makeup and dressing in fashion.

Peter was only nineteen when his parents died. He came home to take over the running of an estate he hardly knew. His qualifications were the captaincy of the school cricket team. He said he was the best batsman the school had ever had and, although this did not mean he could go to university, most people in the village were impressed. He assumed the management of the farm, but without support. It was I who told him what scoundrels the local workers were. Whilst I arranged the vases of flowers in each room, he would follow me around. I explained how much he needed someone who knew the village families to watch over their work. It was not long before I was watching over him.

It was not until after our marriage that I noticed how creepy Mel had become. He was blind and his father had been the estate beekeeper. Mel learnt the skills and made enough money to keep a very tidy little house in the village. Most afternoons would see him climbing the hill to work on his private hives by the wood but, like his father, he also worked the hives on the estate. He always walked like a ghost in the early evening – so softly that you could not hear him until he was beside you. Before Peter and I were married, Mel had approached Peter and negotiated a deal to keep the estate honey in the conservatory at a ridiculously low rent. Mel was probably laughing all the way to the bank as he kept most of what he got for selling Peter's honey.

I warned Peter about Mel; but Peter did not seem to feel that he was losing out. Then I told him how uncomfortable I felt when Mel was about. "I sense he's watching every move I make. I hate how he prowls about in the twilight. I do not like him. He smells of syrup. He wears netting around his face. It's like having a burglar stalking around the estate." Peter told me I was being melodramatic. He even ignored me when I pointed out how vulnerable I felt as a woman with this scary little man near me so often. Peter does not understand a woman's intuition.

Peter's drinking companion, Jack, had been one of the village youths who paraded about the convent school. He had gone over to Greece to receive his police training and had returned as the local law officer. He is much bigger than Peter with heavily muscled shoulders from which his revolver swings. The last time I warned Peter of my fears about Mel, Jack was present. "If he causes you any trouble, just tell me and I'll sort him out," Jack told me. I found this more reassuring than Peter's studied indifference to the danger I was in. But in the two years since our marriage, Peter seems to have lost interest in everything. He could not understand how the estate lost money although I told him if he left me in charge of the finances all that would change. He had started drinking more since Jack came back to the island. And, as I had not become pregnant, he kept moaning that I ought to go to England for tests.

I was raped the night of the bacchanalia – our village summer festival. Jack had brought Peter home. Both had drunk a lot, but Peter was talking incoherent rubbish about no-one on the island knowing how to bowl a ball. I thanked Jack for bringing Peter home and led my swaying husband up the stairs. Later, in bed, I heard a noise in the conservatory outside. Peter was snoring but I was suddenly angry. It was one thing for Mel to move his honey pots in the evening, but the sun had set, and he should respect this as the time when civilised people sleep. I decided to confront him there and then. Not even stopping to pull on a dressing gown (after all he could not see me with nothing on but my night dress) I stormed over to the conservatory. It was in total darkness, so I shouted out; "Mel, come out here immediately." He did not come out, but I heard him moving around. I walked in to switch on the light.

It was not until I was inside the conservatory that I remembered that there was no light. Suddenly I was pushed forward over the workbench. A powerful arm pressed me down. I could smell the honey as I struggled to get free. But his arm was far too strong, and I could not move. "Let me go, Mel," I screamed as I felt him bring his whole body up against my legs which he was forcing apart. I realised that he must have been waiting for me as his penis thrusts banged me up and down. My suspicions about him were being fully realised but now it was too late to ask for Jack's protection. When he had finished with me, he gave a deep groan and pushed me off the bench. Crying, I ran from the conservatory and back to the house – locking the door in case Mel tried to follow me. I rushed up to the bedroom and tried to rouse

Peter who was still in a deep sleep. Frustrated at his inability to wake up, I grabbed the phone and dialled the police station. There was no answer, and I did not know Jack's home number.

I stopped for a moment. I felt dirty and hurt. My husband was just lying there – as useless now as he was as an estate manager. I ran to the kitchen and filled a saucepan with cold water. Peter woke with a start as the full force of the water hit him. "Wake up, you slob!" Peter jumped up with both arms raised as if expecting to be hit. "I told you I was afraid, and you did nothing. I told you Mel was after me and you did nothing. And now that devil has raped me in the conservatory whilst you lie here in a drunken stupor. Are you going to do nothing now?"

Peter leapt to his feet, staring at the wall. He did not look at me; his eyes seemed to bore their way through the house, out across the fields to where Mel lived. Still wearing only his shorts, he strode across the floor, seized his beloved cricket bat, and walked to the door. "I won't let the team down," he shouted as he unlocked the front door and moved off down the hill. In the hour before he returned, I tried to find Jack's home number in Peter's diary: and searched for the local phone directory in vain. I took a shower and washed away the dirt: then I felt ill and was violently sick. I tried to control a terrible fit of sobbing and, eventually, grabbed the saucepan that still lay on the bed and marched across to the conservatory. Without thinking, I threw open the door and flung the saucepan inside. It crashed into a ceramic pot that splintered on impact. The sticky contents could be heard dripping through the split for hours into the next day. I ran back into the house and locked the door. Worrying about what might happen to Peter, I tried phoning Jack at the police station again. It was then that I heard Peter shouting for me to unlock the door.

I asked him what had happened as he walked in with his bat carried triumphantly over his shoulder. "I think we won," he said smiling. I grabbed him and whispered; "Let's phone Jack and tell him what Mel did to me." Peter agreed and picked up the receiver. My voice sounded strange to me as I spoke. "I tried phoning the police station, no-one answered." Peter just dialled his friend's home number and said "Hello Jack. I think you should come up here and sort out a little trouble we've been having. Ann has been attacked by Mel and I've given him a good hiding."

Justice demands that I receive a substantial financial award for the abuse I have suffered. But, worst of all, I cannot bear to think that I might be carrying a beekeeper's child.

2. PETER'S STORY

The island was a holiday retreat when I was a child. It was a place where my parents would bring me to escape the cold winters of England. Its colours were bright and clear whilst England was drab and wet, but its traditions and responsibilities were as strong as England's, and I was born to bear these. I never thought I would have to assume them so young; but I come from family bred to rule and so I never shirked my duties.

At school, the English traditions of fair play work were enforced with an iron discipline. Everyone benefited from strict codes by which we lived. It was not until I was in my final years that I got used to the routine of waking up the boys who were not too bright with a bucket of cold water and a few slaps around the head. By then, I was in the cricket team and playing so well that the school was proud of my achievements. I was never too good at numbers in class, but I could certainly pile on the runs when I was at the crease. My greatest regret since taking over the estate is the lack of any cricket on this Greek island.

I have often wondered how my father managed the family's finances so well. His collection of ancient pottery depicting various Greek myths is meant to be worth a lot of money although I could never understand the stories. He seemed to spend most of his time away from home, yet the estate worked well, and my mother said she never lacked for anything. The school fees were paid promptly. I knew this as the boys whose fees were outstanding used to have their names called in assembly – but mine was never on the list. When I eventually have a son and heir, I am not too clear about how we shall manage to pay the fees. For some reason, the crops do not seem to bring in the wealth to which my family is accustomed. Ann says it is because I am too generous to the labourers. Jack said is it's because I drink French brandy instead of the local ouzo. I cannot figure it out myself, although I suspect Mel of ripping me off on the honey storage deal.

Ann shocked me when she told me of Mel's stalking. I have always seen Mel as a rather harmless fellow who liked to be around the farm gathering in the honey. But Ann insisted that she knew about the local men, and she did not trust him. And Ann has always been the woman who will bring me my son and heir soon. She looks unlike any other woman on the island. With her delicate skin and long red hair, she reminds me of the reproduction pre-Raphaelite portrait that used to hang in my house master's study at school. Although Greek was her native tongue, she seems more like an English princess who ruled my heart once my mother passed away.

Ann was always the gentlest soul. She was the lady of flowers, and I always picture her as holding a glorious bunch of marigolds or a sprig of geraniums in her dainty hands. She even persuaded me to plant flowers as a crop in one field in our first year of marriage. She felt sure she could sell them to tourists: but most withered in the sun before a single drachma passed into the account. So, I have kept Ann away from the harsh world of business since then. A couple of times in the past year has seen her trying to persuade me to hand over the finances: but my housemaster always said that a woman's place was in the home as the female does not have the head for figures. She even tried to convince me that I was not capable of running the business because I drank too much. In this she went too far. Every man deserves the occasional drink, and I am no exception. I can stop drinking at any time I choose so I am no alcoholic. When Ann accused me of this, I felt betrayed.

All the subsequent accusations about Mel were, I felt, an attempt to justify her feeling of insecurity. After all, she knew she had gone over the top in saying I was a drunk; so now she was trying to tell me that others paid her more attention that I did. But after a few drinks with Jack, the troubles of the day seem to fade as we joke about the ways of the world and the island. There is a natural order of things in this world and Jack seems to understand that. When I spoke with Mel in the day, he always seemed most friendly and respectful. So, on the night when Ann told me of his appalling crime, I was more than shocked. As she woke me, I half expected the usual slaps around the head that would follow the soaking. Immediately I knew my duty and I took the bat for my next innings. The long march to the wicket was like a dream where the warm night air wafted me to where I had to be. The game had finally come to the island. Mel opened the door and said how unexpected and welcome a visitor I was. He invited me in, and I executed a perfect hook shot across his ribs. As he bent double, I drove his head through the covers – a splendid boundary for which any batsmen should be applauded. He fell and I could not see him in the darkness. I waved my bat in the air to acknowledge the adulation of the crowd and declared the innings. My walk back to the pavilion seemed longer and the breeze from the sea felt more chill. By the time I got back to Ann, I needed another brandy to steady the nerves. But Ann insisted that I phone Jack first – which seemed only fair as it is considered quite bad form to drink alone.

3. MEL'S STORY

The island is full of sound. The early chatter of the finches up the wooded hill echoes across the farmland waking up to the noisy pair of cocks who call to each other in adjacent fields. The hooded crows settle on the treetops and the insistent 'peep-peep' from the nearby wheatear nest warns of prowling felines far below. I usually get up to the sound of the delivery lorry as it chugs down the hill towards the village shop. If the wind is shaking the trees, I may not hear the clink of the bottles until the crates are unloaded.

In the summer, the air is so clear that you can hear the goats on the hillside fields beyond the wood. Dogs start barking once people are up: they are lazy creatures without the independent spirit of most animals. In the tourist season, the ferry sounds its klaxon at 7.0 a.m. to warn the scurrying couples that the boat leaves in thirty minutes. They call their children in English or German: none of them speak a word of Greek. The church bell tinkles quietly and the old women – six in our village – dutifully clack their way up the street in their heavy winter shoes that they wear all the year round.

The warm air lies still around the hives. I maintain a set near the foot of the hill so the bees can suck the wildflowers in the wood. Their honey has a sharper tang than the honey I draw from the set on Peter's estate. It fetches a better price than the sweet pots I store in his conservatory. So, it is worth the extra work and walk up the slope. If it were not for Peter's voice, I would have given up the honey storage on the estate as I lose money every year working on that hopeless patch. Of course, I can hear Ann even when she thinks I am out of earshot. Her shrill tone can be heard hundreds of metres away. She believes that she knows how to run Peter's business affairs: and she is certain that I am making a fortune from the estate's honey. But she is a foolish and ignorant woman who has dominated the gentle Peter and turned him into a pathetic shadow of his former self.

Even though she was brought up by the nuns and never knew her parents, Ann has always been a spoilt brat. She would scheme and connive even as a child and has never altered in her ways. I still hold her responsible for the loss of my sight, although nothing could be proved. I remember the playground where, as seven-year-olds, we used to invent games. In this summer, some boys brought little water pistols, and we pretended to be cowboys in the American wild West. Jack and I were the leaders of two gangs who would charge around until the school bell called us to order. Some children could not afford the water pistols so would fill up empty detergent bottles with water to squirt their enemies on their clothes. The sun would dry out the clothes by the time we got to the classroom. It was Ann who told Jack that she would favour whichever gang leader got rid of the rival. Jack never brought a water pistol but used a bleach bottle. When he sprayed the contents in my face the next day, the bottle contained only bleach. After several months in hospital, I was eventually sent to a special school on the mainland where blind children were taught.

In the holidays, my father took me around the hives. The world of the bees is complex. On the one hand the reproduction process is ruthlessly efficient, though fatal to the male. After the drone mounts the queen to insert his endophallus, he ejaculates his semen and then drops with his endophallus ripped out of his body by the queen. The emasculated drone dies very quickly with his abdomen burst open. On the other hand, my father showed me how the venom of the bee could help cure arthritis, injuries like tendonitis, and soften keloid and other scar tissue. Before he died, he even started to correspond with researchers who believed that bee venom therapy could help alleviate multiple sclerosis.

At the hives I discovered how creatures co-operate and build even though, like me, they are small and weak. Identifying with the bees has always been easy. As a boy I never wore protective netting when we were at the hives by the wood. My father would say " he loves the bees, and the bees love him." I have never been stung up by the woods as the bees gather wildflower nectar. Only on the estate have I ever had to wear netting as the bees there have always treated nearby movement as a threat. Their sensitivity is even more acute than my hearing as they would start to buzz angrily if Peter approached before I heard his quietly assured gait. Then I would move away to speak with him as he seemed blithely unaware of the danger by standing so close to the hives.

It was his voice that captivated me. A vibrant tenor with a quirky little laugh, he encapsulated all the beauty and insecurity of youth. He seemed awkward if I touched him to shake his hand; but I found myself fantasising on many occasions how it would be if he did permit me to touch him more. I would search for and discover tasks required on the estate to increase the probability of our meeting. It was here that I overheard Ann saying bad things about me in her poor English that she believed I could not understand. Peter seemed to disbelieve her foul slanders ... at least so I thought until he beat me.

The night he came was very still and I heard him walking quickly towards my house. It did not seem a threatening rush; just Peter's soft and regular step that he would take when he was going about a routinely pleasant task. I went to the door, a little excited. I opened it in time to greet him and ask him in. I remember a tremendous pain in my ribs, followed by a blow to my head.

The next thing I knew was hearing Jack's voice. He told me that I was in hospital but that I would recover from Peter's furious attack. He asked me if I knew why Peter would have done such thing. I told him about Ann's ridiculous accusations. He asked if I had ever held any bad thoughts towards Ann. I told him that I had once imagined setting a swarm up her knickers so that the pain she suffered might sting her conscience for her part in my blinding. Jack said he understood and that, in the circumstances, such wealthy people should be made to pay compensation for any harm they had caused me. But he had to ask if I could counter the specific accusations of sexual assault that she had made for the night I had been attacked. I felt extremely light-headed as Jack spoke. I sensed that, in some way, he was trying to apologise and rid himself of the guilt he must have carried around with him since he had squirted the bleach bottle. I told him of my feelings for Peter and my disgust for Ann. Jack wrote my statement and promised to prosecute the case quickly once I had signed it. I did this with some help, and he told me to relax and get well again soon.

4.JACK'S STORY

The island is a battleground. Only those who learn to fend for themselves survive. My father smacked my face if I answered him back as a kid: he said he was the boss and he would stand no little sods giving him any lip. My mother usually kept quiet: she knew she'd get bruised if she said anything. Whenever there were fights at school, my father would say; " if you don't learn to win battles, how can you expect to win any fucking wars?"

Everyone respected my father. He was a real man. Tall in his police uniform, women liked to be near him, and he liked to be near them. He used to boast to my mother that there was scarcely a marriage bed in the island that he had not visited whilst the husband was away. And he liked to know all the gossip. When I came back from the Police Training Academy, he said; "Every good cop knows all the gossip. You need to know what the bastards are up to and who is screwing who." So, I get to know what's happening here as part of my job.

The village families look up to Peter like they used to look up to his parents. But his old man had real money. To get it he used to be off around the world for months – or even a year – at a time. His banking job was where the family fortune came from: the estate always lost money. Whilst he was away his wife would try to break her boredom by pretending to be busy on the farm. But the only good worker there was Aristæus, Mel's father, who got a good business going with bees. But his pathetic son could never make a go of it after he came off worse in a fight with me at school.

Although Peter is a pale shadow of his father, he does own the estate and whilst I was at the Academy, he got Ann – the lucky bugger. She looks like no other tart on the island. They are all dark and hairy; she's smooth and shiny – a lot like Peter's mother. Anyway, I made it my business to be around the estate, picking up the tittle-tattle and chatting up Ann to see what was what. And Peter was always generous with his drink and spilt the beans on the goings-on when he'd had a few. Mind you, his Greek is so bloody awful that I think he gets half the stories wrong anyway. But I like to hear Ann talking – she certainly speaks my language.

The night when Ann alleges the rape took place, I had been drinking with Peter. He said Ann was keen to get more money out of Mel for the honey storage. Of course, I know Mel has as no more money to give them – just as they could not afford to pay the compensation he could claim for Peter's attack. Anyway, I take all this into account when considering why people behave the way they do. As a policeman, you need to be quite a philosopher as well as handy with your fists. Ann was sure that Mel had had his way with her, so I went to interview him. Peter had left him unconscious, so I took the poor sap to hospital. The doctor told me that even if he regained consciousness, there was no way they could save his life as a huge blood clot had formed near his brain.

Fortunately, the little creep did wake up and spilt his guts about his disgusting leching after Peter. Any pervert like that was likely to be guilty of any of the sexual deviations we all learnt about from the Police Academy. So, I had him make a full confession which he signed just before he died. I shall now send Peter over to the mainland for trial on a murder count whilst Ann will have to find a stronger man to support to her on my island.

LUCKY LUKE

To say Luke was lucky would be the understatement of the century. When only eight years old, he joined his friends to walk amongst the visiting holidaymakers along the seafront. At the end of the pier, they were excited by the noise of the crowds, the piped music and the screams of those enjoying a ride on the giant switchback. Luke had a few coins his mum had given him to spend at the fair. The children wandered into the slot machine hall where Luke deposited his first coin. Instantly winning a jackpot was greeted by cheers from his friends.

"Play again, Luke!" they called.

He walked to the next machine that was called 'Find the Lady'. The immediate appearance of three lady pictures in a row – another jackpot – attracted the attention of the grizzly manager who shooed the kids out of the hall.

"I don't know how he did it," the manager told the local journalist later in the day, "but we could not afford the losses that kid was going to impose on us. I suspect he has some sort of magnet to control the levers in the machines."

Luke handing his mum his day's winnings brought a broad smile to her face. She worked part time for her uncle, a popular shoemaker and repairer who could only afford to pay her a pittance. But, under guidance from his niece, he later fashioned a pair of shoes for Luke with a hidden cavity within which valuables could be secreted. This pair of shoes would play an important role in subsequent events: but, at the time, Luke and his mum did not know how.

Mother would not admit to Luke (and certainly not to the journalist) that the winnings were a welcome addition to an overstretched household budget. Luke's father was a poorly paid office clerk who had neither the confidence, nor the talent, to claim a better salary. He allowed himself just one luxury – tobacco for his pipe – but could only afford to award himself one smoke every other day. His wife kept news of Luke's winnings well away from her husband. Luke and his mum formed a secret society that eventually became devoted to exploiting Luke's winning talent.

Father was required to attend a monumentally boring weekend course away from home. All staff were being instructed how to behave by the Bank's Training Director (who, subsequently, ended up in prison after stealing the bank's money!). Father never found out about his wife and son investing in a ticket to the nearby racecourse.

"Which horse do you fancy will win, Luke?"

Excited by the ground shaking fury of a bunch of galloping horses, Luke just said the first word that came into his head. He had no idea from where the word originated as he did not know the names of the horses and riders. But his mum realised that the word invariably described the winner of the next race. Their winnings were more than the household budget for the coming month! On leaving the racecourse, the banknotes were carefully placed within Luke's custom-made footwear.

His mum swore Luke to secrecy about his "God-given talent". Her evening prayers, made in silence after her son was safely tucked up in bed, were focused upon thanking whatever spirit was responsible for this divine intervention in their family's fortunes. She opened a separate bank account to the one she and her husband held for household necessities. Luke was too young to be a signatory, and she had no intention of involving her husband whose intervention she suspected might destroy their son's magical gift.

At school, Luke was a popular boy. He was bright and learned easily, which is why the teachers all liked him. But he did not make a show of his intelligence, which is why his classmates liked him. In the essential boyhood battleground where true value was measured, he was a reasonable although not outstanding performer at football. And as he grew older, girls liked him for his good looks and quiet sense of humor.

The girl whom he liked in return was lovely Linda. The only question that he asked himself was whether his capacity for good luck would extend to winning Linda's affection that was sought by virtually all the other boys of their age.

"Why not ask her if she would like to come to tea?" Luke's mum suggested. Embarrassed, he approached Linda who was chatting with all her girlfriends. He summoned up enough courage to address her. The girls all fell silent awaiting Linda's response.

"What time would you like me to come over?" Linda replied and Luke blushed with joy as he stammered the time his mum had specified.

His mother said nothing but was aware of the old saying "Lucky in love, unlucky at cards." So, there was a hidden reason why she introduced card games for Linda, Luke and her to play after tea. She wanted to gauge whether Luke would win over and again at cards. But he did not; so, from that day on, Linda was regarded as the likely daughter-in-law in waiting.

Two more trips to the races ended with the secret bank account boasting more money than her husband earned in a year. The care with which mother secreted their winnings to avoid the attention of thieves and race officials (often the same men) involved Luke visiting the toilet where he would hide the money in the specially constructed shoes fashioned on the uncle's lathe.

It was a difficult year when Luke left school. He was devastated by his father's suicide committed soon after losing his job at the bank. Linda's family were moving so he was sure that he would lose his girlfriend, and his mother confided in him after his dad's funeral that she was unsure how they were going to manage financially without his salary. Luke suggested that he might become a professional gambler, but his mother was concerned that his magical gift might disappear if it had the added responsibilities of maintaining the household rather than just being a bit of fun – lucrative, but essentially, just fun.

She did not need to worry. He left school and persuaded the manager at the bank to employ him. The manager felt guilty as he had been tasked with making the father redundant. He carried around with him the anxiety that he had been too abrupt and that this had led to the poor man's suicide. He felt morally obliged to give Luke the made-up job of internal messenger which the young man accepted with gusto. Luke rapidly gained insights into how stocks and shares were dealt. Using money that his mum gave him from the secret account, he began investing in shares. Within a year, Luke's earnings far outstripped those of the manager who had given him the menial job. But Luke turned up every day to carry out the duties of internal messenger: moving documents from out-trays to in-trays within the building every hour and on the hour. These tasks took less than thirty minutes so this gave him ample time for what his dad would have called "playing the market".

"How do you know which shares to buy?" his mum asked him.

"I don't know," he replied. "I go into my little office and take out the bottle of wine that I keep hidden in my desk. I take a few swigs and become a little giddy. I close my eyes, and the suggestion of a company name appears. It just happens that whenever I purchase shares in that company, the value rises without my doing anything. And after I sell, the share price always falls."

Linda had followed a more academic route and was attending a course at a famous university. But, whenever she had the time, she would travel back to her former hometown to be with Luke. His newfound wealth, she assumed, came from achieving a senior position in the city bank. She had no idea about Luke's gift, and he maintained the secret he shared with his mum.

Even after they were married, Linda was never told about the gift although she was aware that Luke frequently indulged in drinking copious swigs of wine. Even after his mum died and the enormous fortune amassed in the secret bank account was left to Luke, no one knew how the money had been made nor how Luke continued to pile on the money whilst maintaining the appearance of being nothing more than a messenger.

Trouble only started after their son, Sunny, was born. Linda had unwisely confided in her uncle that the custom-made shoes were constructed for carrying Luke's winnings. When her uncle's grandson, Ali, discovered that the shoemaking side of the family left them considerably poorer than the wealth into which Sunny had been born, he claimed entitlement. "How could Luke, a mere messenger, claim to be so rich?"

The dispute as to who had the rights to the massive investment in oil shares that Luke had made centered around the role of what Ali described as the source of their financial security, the carefully fashioned shoes. Ali asserted that without his grandfather's shoes, there would have been no money.

Luke and his mum (as well as the gifted shoemaker) had long since died. The war that broke out between the two sides of the family continues today. Ironically, both sides of the family assert that gambling and the drinking of wine are proscribed evils.

BOOK SIX

MORE JEWISH TALES UNTOLD

The winter in the Mediterranean was over and I had returned to my hometown, settling into an apartment very near where I had been born and raised. Apart from the earlier unplanned meeting with Sachs, I saw none of the Tzadik's students. Every evening, I would sit at my desk and stories seemed to spring forth, unbidden. I did not feel as if I were the storyteller, merely the transmitter of a tale that wanted to be told. Perhaps the Tzadik would approve of this return to my roots – but I no longer cared what he, nor anyone else, might think. To me, these were just more tales, previously untold.

EZRA AND NEHEMIAH

The meeting was extremely unfriendly. I wonder if this is always the case when there a confrontation occurs between people who interpret their common culture differently. Some fundamentalists within my own religion take grave exception to someone who does not faithfully carry out all the rituals associated with our traditions.

My wife was not Jewish. Her father was Sanballat who is commonly regarded as a great enemy of our people. I am not so sure that he was: but there again I am quite biased. But no one could deny my heritage as my dad was the priest, Eliashib. I was named Joiada (literally 'Knowing God') and my family had been dedicated to the building and upkeep of critical areas of our home city, Jerusalem.

When Jews were allowed back to Jerusalem from their exile in Babylon, not everyone made the journey. We regarded many of those who stayed in the security of the Babylonian Empire as frightened of facing the challenges we had endured back in Israel. So, our cultures and practices began to diverge which meant that some, who regarded themselves as carrying "the true faith" in Babylon, saw us as near heretics.

With the authority of the Babylonian ruler, we were visited by one of these fundamentalists, Ezra. He saw our practices as undermining what he understood to be 'true Judaism', and he was determined to stamp them out. Things came to a head when his sidekick, Nehemiah, confronted those of us who had married out, demanding that we divorce our wives and disinherit our children. Of course, I refused.

Because of my exalted position in Jerusalem society, I was pushed forward to argue against the policies being actively pursued by these Babylonian evangelicals (I think you might call them frummers!)

Nehemiah asserted that we were required to marry within the faith. The benefits were obvious to him (although not so obvious to me). There was some degree of security that was expected to come from marrying someone who might often be a relative. Financial stability, marital stability and the ease of transmission of our cultural values and cultural continuity. Keeping a 'close family' reduced uncertainty about how to care for family members as they got old or infirm. But, above all, only a very specific group of close relatives are forbidden to be married together according to Leviticus: otherwise, the authority of Ezra is that all Jews should marry within the Jewish community.

I countered his arguments as best I could. I pointed out that marrying out and having children with a Jew marrying a non-Jew was well documented in our religious texts. Abraham and Hagar had Ishmael. Ruth herself was a Moabite whose first husband, Mahlon, was Jewish even before she shacked up with Boaz. You could hardly call her a 'shicksa' as she was King David's great grandmother! As for Solomon: most of his many wives were not Jewish.

Nehemiah asserted that irrespective of these historical examples, Ezra had declared that 'marrying out' was prohibited – even if this rule had been disobeyed at times. I countered that I was unaware of any such proscription from any sacred text. In fact, my suspicion was that Sarah, who was Abraham's sister, had already observed the unfortunate results of consanguineous marriage. I asserted that our physicians had already noted that the children of such marriages tended to have more heart trouble, cancer, deafness and learning disability. We had seen how brother/sister marriages in Egypt formed to retain a dynasty's 'royal blood' frequently resulted in severely disabled children.

I wondered whether the main reason why our religion had prospered over so many centuries might have been partly due to the prevalence of 'marrying out' which avoided what you would call the genetic disorders associated with inbreeding.

Nehemiah's response was to order his Babylonian armed guards to escort me out only to find that they had executed my wife and children.

"We have to retain purity of blood!" he shouted at me.

PINCHBEC

As a journalist in a provincial newspaper, most of what I wrote were stories of minor floods, local weddings, and controversies over road closures. My wife knew that my ambitions as a writer were pious hopes supported by zero commitment of time and even less interest from publishers. So it was with some surprise that she told me about Harry Pinchbec's visit.

He had called at our house while I was out and told my wife that he wanted to pay me to write his life story. He said he had read my little articles and liked my writing style which he described as "short and to the point." I was not really interested until she told me how much he had suggested as a fee. It was the sort of proposition that I could hardly refuse, and, at any rate, my wife would have threatened divorce if I had turned it down.

He had left an address and phone number: so, I called and arranged to meet him at his home. The house was a two up/two down terrace in an area of the town where poverty was only just below the surface. He opened the door and showed me into a neat room whose furniture was almost certainly twenty or thirty years old. He offered me a cup of tea but as I could just see into the kitchen, where washing up was obviously only undertaken when there were no cups available, I politely refused. He sat down opposite me and, although

I am over average height, he peered down at me. I guessed he was about six and a half feet tall but seemed even taller because he was exceptionally thin. His arms seemed to dangle uncomfortably, and he had a strange twitch that moved his legs apart, then closed, then apart again.

When he spoke, he did not address me directly but let his eyes wander all around the room although there was precious little to see. There was a large mirror just to my right that hung precariously off the wall. He looked at it a lot and I realised it was positioned so that he could see himself. He had a high, nasal voice with a local Midland accent that rasped on the ear. The room smelled of mold. If it were not for the offer of the fee, I suspect I would have been looking for excuses to leave within a few minutes.

Instead, I asked him why he wanted a short biography. He explained that his life had been so interesting that others might want to read about it. I asked him how his life had begun "just so I can see how you grew up and what you achieved afterwards." He said he was an only child, and his father was "in the army." I asked him where he had been stationed, was Harry a child of the war, and which countries he had been to as a boy. He explained his dad worked in the Payments Section ensuring soldiers receive their wages. He had never been stationed anywhere outside England and, truth be told, he could not remember much about him because he had died when Harry was only twelve. Both his parents used to chain smoke and his father's death from lung cancer occurred before the public associated it with smoking.

I asked about his mother, but Harry seemed reluctant to talk about how she had managed as a widow. He implied that as a teenager he rarely knew which man he would find in the house when he got back from school. I asked about relatives. There was only his mum's brother, Patrick, who had emigrated to New Zealand after 1945. The only contact with Patrick had been the receipt of a single condolence card when Harry's mum died a few years later. By the time I left Harry's house, I had obtained a strong impression of a not very happy childhood. It was obvious that the biography would have to highlight how his achievements as an adult were significant as he came from such a poor background.

We had arranged to meet again at a pub where we could chat over a drink. I thought the convivial atmosphere might help him recount all the interesting aspects of his life which he was paying me to describe. When I told my wife about the first encounter she asked, "how old do you think he is?" I shrugged my shoulders and asked what she thought as I always found her much better at those types of guessing games. "About twenty years older than you?" I was quite shocked because I thought he was like me, about seventy, maybe a little younger. But she told me to look at the lines on his forehead and, if possible, look at the back of his hands. "He has never worked physically: but his hands are quite weathered. I would guess he is well into his nineties."

When we were seated in the pub, I watched him raise his pint of beer. The back of his right hand was clearly visible and rather than "weathered" I would have described it as "withered". I sat back and asked him to tell me about his life. I could hardly believe my ears when he responded: "Well, there's not much to tell really. I was hoping you could show it as interesting with your skills as a writer." I sensed that I would have to work hard for my fee. So, I took him back to his school days. "What subjects did you like and what were you best at?" He said that in a class of thirty, he was always about fifteenth – "not too bright but not too bad" was his description. "I was best at arithmetic." I jumped at this and asked if he thought this was because, like his father, his aptitude for sums could serve him well when it came to getting a job. He thought about this for half a minute before saying he had never thought of that. "Perhaps that's why I managed to get the job in the insurance office."

I felt I was just beginning to get a handle on his early life. "Tell me about the insurance office." He said he worked with three other people for many years. His boss, Calvin, was black and laid back. "He was a really nice boss: always willing to help." "Not like some black men I've met," he added. Then there was Jim, the other insurance agent who always wanted to show Calvin that he was better at selling insurance than Harry. And there was Linda, the secretary, who typed up all the documents for clients to sign and kept the office neat and tidy. "So did you like working there?" It seems Harry really fancied Linda and openly disliked Jim. The irony was that Jim and Linda were married to one another. He never socialised with them after office hours. As for Calvin, he was a man totally out of Harry's league when it came to socialising. As a popular jazz trumpeter, he was engaged playing in clubs around the county and said he probably earned more with his band than he ever did for the insurance company.

"What did you do with yourself after office hours when you were a young man?"

"Not much. I used to go to the city to hear orchestral concerts. I really enjoyed them."

At last, I felt I was starting to hear what drove this quiet man when he was starting out. I asked about his taste in music and discovered that he was surprisingly knowledgeable considering that he never played an instrument himself and had never been to classes to learn about the subject. In his understated way, he waxed lyrical about Tchaikovsky and seemed to know a lot about the circumstances of the composers' writing his symphonies. His favourite was number six, which he described in some detail. He said the first time he had heard it, the finale left him physically in tears. If Harry was a true romantic, I wondered how close to the composer he was in other ways.

I broached the subject carefully. "Did you attend the concerts on your own or did you go with a partner, a girlfriend perhaps?" He shook his head. He went alone and had no girlfriends. He disclosed that he had never married and had no children. I asked if he knew how Tchaikovsky's marriage had turned out: I tried to avoid asking straight out if Harry was like his hero, a repressed homosexual. Harry nodded. He knew all about it and said he thought he himself could not possibly be gay as he had really fancied Linda. The subject was clearly embarrassing him, so I moved on quickly to ask about what else he did apart from attending classical concerts.

"I didn't go to university, but I used to take books out the library and read a lot."

I asked which authors he found most engaging and was left with a list that he seemed to be memorising from a sheet of paper that he ticked off with a nod of his head after each name had been called. "T.S.Eliot, Kingsley Amis, Christopher Marlow" then he paused and added "Martin Luther, Matvei Golovinski, Louis-Ferdinand Celine." I found this a puzzling reply but did not know how to follow it up. After all, when it came to writing his biography, I really needed to know more about what he had achieved rather than his reading preferences. As for Matvei Golovinski and Louis-Ferdinand Celine, I had never heard of them.

I bought another round of drinks in the hope he would loosen up and start to divulge the most interesting aspects of his life that would form the core of my account.

"I think I have a rough idea of your background," I began," now I need you to tell me what parts of your life would most engage the reader of your biography."

He sat quiet for a moment, then began wiggling his legs and swaying side to side in an that annoying nervous tic which seemed to accompany any uncomfortable thoughts. He was silent for over a minute. I decided to say something just hoping to get him going.

"What would you like me to highlight in the account, Harry?"

Eventually he stopped fidgeting and looked me in the eye. Finally, instead of his evasions and distracting glances all around the room, he seemed to want to impart something of importance.

"I want you to explain the great secret I have discovered and show how it has helped guide me through my life as I am sure it could for others."

If he had not seemed so serious, I would have guessed that this was a prepared speech before some sort of joke revelation. But I decided to keep quiet and think of the fee rather than worry about Harry's "guide through life". Then he looked me in the eye and said: "If you've read these great authors, you would also see what I can see. They knew the great secret of how our civilisation has been undermined and how we are controlled by the great conspiracy."

I had no idea what he was talking about but, still thinking of my fee, I encouraged him to tell me more.

"I have lived my life in the full knowledge of how all our lives are being controlled by those who hold power over us."

I took a deep breath waiting for an unoriginal, though accurate, account of how far right, super wealthy media owners portrayed immigrants, the poor, anyone but them for the problems meted out to most people. But instead, I received a description that could have come straight from the 'Protocols of the Elders of Zion' (which is when I remembered who Matvei Golovinski was). Harry told me that it was certain that the Jews controlled everyone as they were super rich and owned the countries he listed as America, Israel and – for some reason – Russia, France, Germany, and England. He wanted his biography to highlight how he had come to have these "great truths" revealed to him so that others could benefit from his insights.

I decided to forget about the promised fee.

"Harry. Did you know that I was Jewish?"

With this true revelation, Harry dropped his beer onto his lap; got up, confused; shouted at me that I made him spill his beer; and ran out of the pub.

My wife said it was a shame the fee would never be forthcoming but that I should write an account of what had happened so that others might know about Harry Pinchbec.

INTIFADA

When Neons took over the northern desert, Retros were glad to see them go. It had always been an unhappy co-existence. The Neon refusal to accept Retro gods and their way of life was mirrored by the disgust that Retros felt at what they saw as Neon immorality. Neon daughters making their own decision about who to marry led to a higher rate of divorce than that countenanced by Retro authorities. The removal of many young Neon males as they travelled north made the problem of Retro daughters falling for these purveyors of promiscuity recede into the faraway sands to which Retro girls dared not travel alone. But population displacement always has unanticipated consequences.

The unexpected problem for the northern nomadic Retros feeling pushed out by these new arrivals saw southern Retros divided as to how to treat their nomadic brothers who had then fled south. Some declared that there was no room for these people who steadfastly refused the static caravans they were offered as accommodation. "Send them back!" declared Sanders – the leader of the Retro Party of Religion and Land (the

PRL). Ironically, the identical call was made by the PRL in the north who regarded the incursion by the Neons as an invasion.

Sanders saw himself as the most ardent defender of traditions. His appeal was aimed at anyone who felt threatened by the changes that were occurring in the region. He was assassinated by a right-wing radical who regarded the PRL as "too soft" on the cultural challenge posed by Neons. The fact that Sanders had not been killed by Neons made no difference to political figures who wished to profit by his death. Most of them, and their owned news outlets, irrationally blamed Neons for Sander's murder.

Several decades of conflict followed as Neons who had remained in the south were prevented from taking positions of power and influence. Retros should not have been surprised by the younger generation of Neons rebelling against the oppressive PRL regime and arming themselves against Retro police and far right gangs. Hampered by years of stagnant one-party rule, nepotism and corruption, PRL resistance against the young Neons crumbled. The Neon old guard assumed that the young leader, Yosher, would be content in declaring the northern desert as the Neon Homeland and expelling the Retro surrogates who had been placed there to rule. But Yosher, who had been raised in the south, said that he wanted to unite the north and south as one, undivided nation, to be governed wisely by Neon intellectuals together with sympathetic Retros.

Retro anger was initially repressed in the face of Yosher's appeal. Their problem was that many Retro youngsters (especially young women) saw Neon life as infinitely preferable to what they had been enduring. So Yosher was lauded like a pop star. He was young, successful and – unsurprisingly – the plaudits went to his head. When Retro representation was made, asking for land in the south to be reserved for Retro religious observance, he believed he were doing Retro women a favour by refusing the request. Retros living abroad started arriving to challenge Yosher, who adopted a familiar slogan: "Send them Back".

It was actually Yosher's son, Gideon, who led the most effective campaign against his father. Gideon believed that, although Retro religious observance and social customs were anathema to him personally, there was no reason to believe that Neon culture was superior to Retros.

"We are different, but mutual respect is the basis upon which any peaceful future can be built," he said. Gideon did not possess the instant appeal and charisma of his father, but he managed to bring together the beginnings of a "Peace Movement". He led a high-profile march into a traditional Retro area, bravely attempting to engage those in the Retro community with similar beliefs in how to create a co-existent society.

Sander's grandson met Gideon in what the naïve Neon youngster believed would be the start of a great coming-together of minds and ways of life. When Yosher heard that the meeting had hardly started when Sanders pulled out a gun and shot Gideon "in retribution for the oppression of our people", his anger knew no bounds. Thousands of Retros were killed and dozens of Neons died in the following year.

I have gone to live in the northern desert with my family. We had wanted to follow Gideon but were forced to choose between agreeing with Sanders' demand for justice or Yosher's demand for justice. It was an impossible choice created by historical forces well beyond our control. Even up here, we do not feel safe. I keep a loaded rifle beside our bed at night and my wife always carries a 9-millimeter Glock pistol in her handbag. My daughter wanted to know if I would buy her a gun for her eleventh birthday and my son started his first job working for Sentinel, the company making armed drones. I asked him how he felt about our Retro neighbours who had also travelled north to escape the war. He said, "Send them Back!"

THE INTERVIEW

"You ask why am I here? Well, I'll tell you what happened. I was becoming confused. I went to our rabbi and said that I was not sure that I was a Jew anymore. He asked me what I thought being a Jew was, so I catalogued everything I could think of. Our heads make some of us great mathematicians and philosophers. Our hearts make some of us wonderful musicians and religious leaders. Our history makes us proud and moralistic. Our circumstances make us financially astute and suspicious. Our enemies make us into pariahs – and lampshades. Our religion tries to make sense of it all – but I'm not sure I believe in it. Our rabbi shrugged and asked why I was uncertain whether I was a Jew anymore. I told him about my feelings as more and more thugs were appearing on the streets of Europe –

fear, anger, anxiety. He looked cross and asked if such scum would make me deny my identity. But I told him that it was worse than that. The week before I had denied the Torah itself, I had purchased an automatic rifle for the protection of my family against the neo-Nazis. But then I found myself planning how to use the weapon against enemies even when they were not threatening me. He laughed in relief and said, "Is that all? My dear friend, you have merely become a Zionist." So that is what I am doing here."

The Tel Aviv Immigration Officer yawned, stamped the documents, and called for the next in the queue.

GRAVE INJUSTICE

The problems encountered by the children of Oran were unique. As the ruler of the planet Ob, Oran had been beset by the aftereffects of the strike by the Chew birds. Chew birds had always been happy to dispose of the bodies of Obs by consuming them after they were ceremonially carried to the mountain top above the capital city. But as the pollution worsened in the city, the bodies became inedible. The Chew birds refused to accept the new corpses.

Oran's solution, burying Obs in a graveyard, seemed satisfactory at the outset. But after Oran died, his two children who ruled jointly, were faced with the unprecedented appearance of reincarnated Obs emerging from the graves. Oran's son, Karl, thought that these ghostlike figures could be ignored. They did not interact with the world as they knew it, passing through walls with ease but unable to move objects. Oran's daughter, Princess Sweets, was less sanguine. She felt that these phantoms were so disturbing that the population would not be happy about government inaction. Children and old people were frightened by their sudden appearance. She said it was the duty of those in charge to act.

She persuaded Karl to make a new approach to the Chew birds to discover if there was any way that bodies could be cleaned so that the pollutants which the birds described as disgusting might be removed. But the birds remained unconvinced that any relative of Oran could be trusted. The new rulers' declaration that they would do everything in their power to make the corpses "edible and even tasty" was greeted with disdain. "They wouldn't know how to prepare them with herbs and spices. They seem to think that even stuffing their live bodies with extra hyaluronic acid, injecting the skin with horrible-tasting tattoo ink and decorating them with metal inserts is good for you. How would they know how to prepare a juicy corpse for us?"

Karl decided to take control. He told Princess Sweets to take a back seat whilst he imposed a new requirement on all undertakers to encase coffins with metal. "This will prevent the dead from rising" he explained. Unfortunately, his ignorance was exposed when the new batch of corpses reappeared with metallic fingers with which they were able to short circuit electrical circuits and tap strange, morse code-like messages on wooden or metal surfaces.

Disenchanted with the rule of Oran's children, the people began to form political groupings that sought to bring new ideas about how to control the growing number of ghosts wandering the streets and alleyways of the city by day and night.

In Parliament, the Wrighton Party denounced the Chew birds and decided that they needed to be forced to assume their traditional role of corpse consumer. Declaring war on the birds, the Party's military wing climbed the mountains in search of the nests. Finding only long-deserted eyries, they set fire to the straw and, as the smoke rose, declared that they had defeated the enemy. Unfortunately for the jubilant Henry Wrighton, as he descended the mountain, a couple of very young Chew birds spied him and – feeling peckish – decided to make a meal of him. Sue Ella Wrighton, his daughter, declared that there was obviously a worldwide conspiracy masterminded by the birds responsible for virtually all the problems of society.

When Steve Karma's opposition party declared that the best policy might be to cease tattooing and the practice of sticking metal inserts into various parts of the body so that the birds might resume the age-long practice of corpse disposal, Sue Ella denounced this as an attack on the freedom of expression, the right of every Ob to do, say or act however they liked. Steve Karma responded with an article ridiculing Sue Ella's belief in a worldwide conspiracy of Chew birds. She responded by getting Karl royal support in preventing Steve Karma writing or saying anything against her religious belief in the evil of the Chew birds.

The Obs élite did not like Steve Karma ("too bloody radical") nor Sue Ella (too bloody loving the adoration of ignorant plebs). So, they decided that the best solution was to return to the good old days of Oran. Princess

Sweet's little son, Bo, was too young to understand politics: in fact, even when he eventually grew up, he was too stupid to understand almost anything at all. So, the Obs élite recognised in Bo the ideal ruler whom they could direct. He can still be seen most nights standing on the corner by the palace, chatting inanely to any passing phantom. They do not take any notice of him, and he talks to them like a child would speak to their pet puppy. Under these circumstances, it is not surprising that watching this innocuous performance on television has persuaded the population simply to ignore the profusion of harmless phantoms and go about their business as if the past can be safely ignored. Recently, however, the morse code-like tapping of these ghosts has been deciphered. But no government-controlled media outlet will ever broadcast the messages. Freed from the fear that anything worse can be administered to them, the dead daily list the injustices they suffered before descending into their graves.

THE HUNT

They lived by a beautiful, bathing lake. In the evenings, she enjoyed plunging in. The whole family would come. She had taught her little ones to be strong swimmers. Other families might join them: but they lived at the quiet end of the lake. It was not uncommon for them to see nobody for days.

It was late, the sun was already hot. She had been teaching her youngest how to dive when she heard the sound. It was a sound that is always unmistakable; heavy and clumsy. It was the rustling and rough breathing of a group of men trying to walk quietly. They were some way off, but she felt afraid. It was the fear that made your back feel cold, your feet move faster, your breast tense across shorter, nervous breaths. She had seen groups of men near the lake before. They were loud, they laughed, they left litter. She had hidden behind bushes, and they had walked past, kicking stones, and calling each other to make less noise. She knew that she was safe as long as they could not see her. So, she led the way to a hiding place again.

As they came nearer, she could almost catch the smell of their clothes – damp with perspiration. Their footsteps seemed uncertain; they had no clear direction. They were prowling and dangerous. Her family sensed her fear and had stopped their usual play. She peeped through the undergrowth and froze. The leading man was no ordinary loiterer: he was dark and angry with the World. His face was a mask of contempt. He surveyed the lake, teeming with life, as if it were beneath him – in his possession. What did he want to do with the lake? What did he want to do with her? Suddenly she felt that she could not breathe. She turned and, with a last look at her family, spread her wings to take off. The men raised their rifles to fire.

DEATH IN THE FAMILY

Have you noticed how familiar sounds seem strange when you are ill? How light appears to glimmer where previously there were only shadows? And, of course, you lose your senses of smell and taste.

This was quite serious for me because I was a chef. Curiously, I was not at first aware that I was unwell. It was only when one of my regular customers complained about one of my *pièces de résistance* that I began to suspect that something was wrong. Hesitatingly, I confided in my spouse who told me immediately that this was a lame excuse for my inattention in bed over the previous few weeks.

I can recall events years ago as if they were yesterday. When I was a child and was unhappy, I remember wandering down to an oak that grew nearby. Adults told me that it had been there for over five hundred years. And when no-one was in sight, I would talk quietly to the great trunk, and it would creak its branches in reply. The manager in the nearby hotel says that he tells all his troubles to a psychiatrist whose front room window garishly advertises his services to passers-by. Instinctively, my choice of confidant was probably wiser.

It was a sunny evening when I left our house for a walk that retraced my childhood route. The crickets were more insistently noisy, and car doors seemed to reverberate as breadwinners returned home. The cries of children playing in the park were individually distinguishable and I could hear the brook trickling across rough-strewn stones beyond the busy road. I stopped to sniff the aroma of the wallflowers that guarded the park wall, but I could not smell anything.

The tree had a little fence erected to protect it from people carving their names on its bark. The surrounding ground had become overgrown with untended scrub. I stopped beside the fence and carefully surveyed the area. I did not want to look ridiculous if I spoke to my tree. But the place was deserted.

Have you ever been surprised? No, I don't mean surprised as when a friend unexpectedly turns up. Or when a tureen crashes to the floor as the sous-chef concocts his first hot soup. No, I mean when you open your mouth to say something to a tree and it speaks instead.

"Listen," the oak said. My mouth stayed open. This was not imagination; the voice was as clear as my memory of childhood.

"Look across the park." I did as I was told.

"You see the wind?" And I saw the air currents as the specks of dust were carried up close by the road, and down again over the grassy banks.

"Now smell the flowers." I drew in my breath deeply, and for the first time for many weeks, I could sense the various plants as if they were laid out before me.

"Now touch my bark." I stretched my arm through the fence but could not reach.

"Climb over, you need to feel it." Clumsily, I hauled myself over the railing and pressed my hands against the trunk. The branches creaked knowingly.

The family had gathered around the tree.

"I wonder what he was doing down here."

"He never said anything to me about meeting anyone."

"No, I don't think he was seeing anyone; he just needed inspiration to continue to invent those wonderful dishes."

"Yes, but what's inspiring about this awful place?"

"Nothing. But the psychiatrist thought his patient's plaque should be welded to the railings: 'To our greatest chef'."

"Perhaps coming down here helped him through the stresses of managing his restaurant."

"Only the tree would know the answer to that."

We all walked back across the crisp carpet of golden leaves, freshly laid.

AT THE CROSSROADS

I have a good reputation as a fiddle player. Most of my work is playing klezmer at Jewish weddings; but every now and again a lucrative summons by a local Christian dignitary puts extra food on the table for my wife and children. When Lady Mary died in a town not far from my village, she left the house and most of her money to her only son, Paul. But she also put aside a sum for the Town Council to organise a celebration after her funeral. So, I was pleasantly surprised to receive an invitation from the Council to play solo fiddle at the event.

I arrived by cart soon after the funeral had finished. The mayor led me to the centre of the town where one cart-track crossed another. "We want you to play here," he pointed to the very centre of the crossroads. "We have set up a gallery for all the townsfolk to listen to your performance," he pointed to a rough arrangement of benches where people had started to gather. At that moment, an immaculately dressed man appeared from the big house to the left of the benches. He shouted at me; "We don't need you here. Go away! You and your high prices, your sales tax ... just leave us alone." The mayor smiled, embarrassed. "You must forgive Paul. He is very upset."

Paul continued his tirade. "Why do you charge us sales tax? Eh, Jew. Answer me that." I called back; "It's not my tax, it's your government's. And they charge it because I am a Jew ... I don't want it."

"Well, we don't want you," he shouted. "We never asked you to be here."

"Yes, you did. And here I am". Someone restrained Paul ... I think it may have been his wife. The mayor could see that his "gallery" was nearly full. So, he suggested that I begin.

"Yes," shouted Paul as he retreated into the doorway of his house. "Show us just how good you are!"

I began with a tricky little piece – a skocne that showed off quick fingerwork to the crowd. Paul listened to the serpentine line writhing its way desperately away from the physical limitations of dance into a realm of intense feeling. The next piece brought him back to earth as the lilt of a hora reminded him of the smiles and movement of his beloved mother when she was much younger. A couple of pieces later, and the haunting nigun with its slow pace and telling silences brought tears to his eyes – the ones that he found he could not shed during the funeral ceremony. The final freylachs asserted that life must go on despite the pain of our joint experiences.

"You filthy Jew," Paul screamed as he rushed towards me with a stick. "Stop playing, will you?" He struck me on the arm and back as I protected my precious fiddle from his tearful attack. He was led away as the mayor came up and apologised again. The audience, who had clapped enthusiastically during and after every number, started to disperse. The mayor handed me the handsome fee and I left for home.

Since then, I have always found it safer to play to people who do not really hear the music.

TROLLEY

At our Girls' School, there were always rumors about parents, gossip about boyfriends (real and imagined) and debates about who were the worst and best teachers. So, it was no surprise when my friends Helen and Gayle informed me that a new girl, Rebekah, was quite peculiar.

"She is not like us," Helen began. "She only attends during the day. She says she would never want to be a boarder like us."

"Who does she think she is?" Gayle joined in. "Does she think her home is a palace so she wouldn't want to lower herself to sleep in our dormitory?"

"I don't know," I replied. "Has anyone asked her?"

Clearly this was not the response my friends wanted. I had to admit that at first sight Rebekah did seem a bit strange. First, she was tiny. Walking along beside her, she barely reached up to my shoulder and I am only average height. Secondly, in class she seemed to be streets ahead of any of us when it came to answering questions. I always struggled with languages, but she responded to questions in French from Mademoiselle Lily like a native speaker. Helen was poor at maths but felt humbled and then antagonistic when Rebekah, sitting beside her, offered to show her how to answer the puzzle. Thirdly, although she had a pretty girl's face, her voice was as low as a boy's. Finally, her clothes were so old-fashioned that Gayle could not resist the temptation to tease her about her long dress. The dress swept along the ground and had long sleeves that stretched beyond her wrists and covered half her hands.

"Perhaps she thinks she is going to set a new trend in clothes: so retro that its retro-retro!"

But Rebekah just smiled at these taunts and, every day, trundled up to school in her all-covering dress. In retrospect, I wonder whether we were all a tiny bit jealous of her. She may have been small, but she had the sweetest face with beautiful black hair that reached down to just above her waist. Her academic work was top rate, but she had permission to miss anything sporty. This should have made us suspicious but none of us realised what she was hiding beneath her dress. We just assumed that although she was clever, she must have some disability that prevented her from participating in athletic activity.

It was Helen who broached the subject before the end of term. Although most weaknesses could be used as reasons to tease, without knowing whether she even had a disability it seemed unnecessarily bitchy to bait the girl about her absence from the hockey pitch.

"You must miss not being able to take part in team sports," Helen said. But Rebekah just smiled and did not reply. This was foolish if she wanted to close the subject down as it just provoked further questions. It was not that we were inquisitive. I suspect that none of us were intelligent or creative enough to have become truly inquisitive. Instead, we were just looking for reasons to bring down a girl whom we felt saw herself as superior to us all.

It was Gayle who felt driven to take matters further. She had her eyes set on a boy who lived in the school. He was the teenaged son of the groundman and helped his father paint white lines on the pitches and collect leaves that blew across the front of the classroom block. He was shy but Gayle had learnt his name was Tom and tried to find any excuse to speak with him in passing. It was obvious to Helen and me that Tom had no interest in Gayle: quite the contrary, when he saw her coming, he would make his way quickly to his dad as if he needed to talk with him about work.

It was something of a shock to Gayle the day she saw Tom chatting to Rebekah. She was speaking and he was responding with smiles and laughter. They were enjoying each other's company. They seemed happy and innocent and at ease with one another. Gayle was furious. "What can he possibly see in that dwarf?" she shouted. Helen and I knew that an explosion was inevitable, but we could never have foreseen what would happen.

Lessons for the day had ended and Rebekah was preparing to leave the school to go home. She had reached the gates when Gayle confronted her.

"What do you think of Tom?" Gayle demanded. Rebekah stopped and looked genuinely puzzled. Helen and I walked over, curious to see how Rebekah would deal with the angry, jealous Gayle.

After a few moments, Rebekah caught Gayle completely off guard with her reply.

"How do you know my brother?" she asked.

Gayle looked over to us, unable to take in what Rebekah had said. So, I butted in: "Rebekah, we did not know you had a brother named Tom. How old is he?"

"Tom is ten years old. I just did not know that Gayle had ever met him."

"I have never met your brother," Gayle went on. "I was talking about Tom, the son of our groundman."

Suddenly the full realisation of what was being asked dawned on Rebekah. She studied Gayle's face and saw how feelings of anger and jealousy contorted the muscles around her mouth. She looked into Gayle's eyes, barely able to control tears that were forcing themselves down her cheeks. It was obvious to Helen and me that Rebekah had no idea how to handle the situation. She might have been very clever academically, but was unused to dealing with a ferociously angry, totally irrational, childishly self-centred youth, intent upon meting out punishment to someone whom she had decided was her worst enemy.

I know, now, years later, that Gayle was behaving no better and no worse than her parents and most adults that she had known. They were wealthy, had a large 4-wheel drive car, and believed that the world owed them a living. They regarded anyone who stood in their way as mere impediments to be mowed down and obliterated so that they could carry on living their lives of luxury. Gayle just saw Rebekah as an enemy to be taken out: so, she attacked her physically.

Before Helen or I could intervene, Gayle grabbed Rebekah by her shoulders and pushed her. She expected her to topple over, but Rebekah just retreated noiselessly. Furious, Gayle grabbed her hands that protruded through the sleeves of her long dress. I was behind Gayle when her hair suddenly seemed to stand on end. In fact, she had received a mild electric shock from tiny implants in Rebekah's wrists. But Gayle did not realize what had happened. So, she stepped back and then charged, head down, aiming at Rebekah's chest. On impact, Rebekah cried out to stop; but Gayle persisted in the assault. She pulled at the long dress and tore the front. Then she thrust her hands below Rebekah's waist to wrestle her to the ground. It was at that moment that she received the devastating electric shock that threw her across the gate and into the wall. She slumped to the ground. Rebekah looked at her and then looked up at us as we stood, open-mouthed, at what we could see.

Gayle had ripped off the front of Rebekah's dress. The tear revealed the reason why she was short and why she could not participate in sport – she had no legs. Just below her waist was a trolley upon which her body rested. Below the trolley, a complex piece of electronic gear was suspended and below that were two rollers instead of feet. She was desperately trying to gather the remains of her dress around her so that none of what she later called her "undercarriage" could be seen. But she knew that Helen and I had discovered her carefully concealed secret that, once seen, could never be forgotten.

"Is she alright?" Rebekah asked, pointing at Gayle who remained prostrate beside the school gate. I went over to see but was not at all confident that she was alright.

Helen shouted to a teacher who had just emerged from the building.

"There's been an accident. I think Gayle might need an ambulance."

The teacher took one look at Gayle, who was unconscious, and started calling the emergency services on her mobile phone. While she was talking to the call handler, Helen and I stood in front of Rebekah so no one else could see what Gayle had revealed. Rebekah managed to cover up her trolley by rearranging her torn dress and looked up at us.

"I don't really want everyone knowing what you've just seen. I would like to keep my physical condition private."

"That's fine by me," Helen said. "But how are we going to explain what happened to Gayle?"

"I know," I piped up. "Couldn't we just say we think she got a shock from static electricity that had built up when she rubbed up too hard against your dress?"

Helen did not look convinced but as neither she nor Rebekah had a better idea, that is what we told the ambulance crew who wondered why Gayle seemed to have suffered an unexplained, severe electric shock. The teacher was similarly dubious about our story: but we stuck with it to help Rebekah keep her secret.

The next day, with Gayle still in hospital, Rebekah took Helen and I aside before lessons began. "Thanks for staying quiet about how Gayle got a shock from sticking her hands into my wiring. Since you've seen how I transport myself around, I think you should know how this has come about. The explosion that killed my mum and dad also wrecked my legs. Tom was unhurt but we were both adopted by a couple who had no children. They are research scientists with the expertise to have created my undercarriage. It took two years before I was able to control the apparatus through my neural network."

"What's that?" I asked.

"It's how my brain sends messages down to the electronic wiring that Gayle stuck her hand into. It automatically defends itself against intrusion by pulsing an electric shock – I cannot control that."

Full of curiosity, Helen asked; "How fast can you move on those rollers?"

Rebekah smiled. "I try to ensure that I always move at the same speed as pedestrians, so I don't draw attention to myself. But I am sure that, if there were an emergency, my rollers could spin me up to over eighty kilometres an hour!"

"This electronic brain you keep down there," I began: "can you use it to calculate and remember stuff we learn in class?"

Rebekah shook her head. "No, it's the brain in my head that is good at maths and remembering the arguments surrounding important events in history. But the electronics controlling my rollers can remember routes taken and has a radar sensor that allows it to guide me even when I am not attending to navigation. When I roll up to school every morning, I just let the rollers take me here and the sensors ensure that I do not find myself crossing a road when cars are coming."

Helen and I were enthralled at what we had discovered about our school friend. But Rebekah was more worried about what was going to happen to Gayle.

"How is she? Do you know if she will be coming out of hospital soon?" she asked. The answer arrived a fortnight later. Gayle walked into school as if nothing had happened. Her memory seemed to have been affected. She was a completely changed character.

"I reckon the shock to her brain has made her into a new woman," Helen said.

"Perhaps so," I replied, "And to be honest, I think it's made her into a much nicer person. She even talks with Rebekah respectfully. I don't think she remembers anything at all about what she did."

It might have remained peaceful if Mademoiselle Lily had not been drunk one night. Although Helen, Gayle and I were not present when it happened, Gordon Jones, a young journalist who worked for the local newspaper, witnessed the event. Lily had emerged from a downtown bar after falling out with her boyfriend. She was upset and had consumed almost a whole bottle of wine after he had stormed out over something that displeased the nasty little man. Dressed in revealing clothes that were already dishevelled, she started lurching down the road back towards her little flat in the school. She caught the attention of two older men who were leaning on the wall opposite the bar. They spoke with one another before deciding to follow Lily. At the end of the road, they accosted her physically. Gordon had emerged from the bar and witnessed what happened at the end of the street. One man got hold of Lily from behind whilst the other began pulling up her dress.

Rebekah happened to be trundling along near Gordon. She looked up and saw Lily being attacked about a hundred meters away. It took only a few seconds before she struck the front man at about fifty mile per hour with her trolley. He went flying and his partner took one look at Rebekah before deciding to run away as fast as he could. Lily was upset but had no idea how Rebekah had arrived so quickly. Gordon, on the other hand, felt he was bound to investigate but the article appearing the next day did not give away Rebekah's secret. Gordon himself had had a fair amount to drink after his evening in the bar, so he was unclear about what he had just seen. The report just spoke of a disabled young woman's bravery in preventing her teacher being raped. A photographer appeared at the school at the end of the week asking if he could have a picture of the heroine so that they could run a full article about her. Helen, Gayle, and I blocked him and explained that there could be no more media coverage. We made up a story that the police had advised that no photos should appear in case the men or their mates tried to take revenge.

Gordon Jones reappeared soon after and we palmed him off on Gayle who took a shine to the enthusiastic young man. Gayle became Gayle Jones a couple of years later, so Helen and I think Gordon got a lot more than if he had just interviewed Rebekah!

Throughout her school career, Rebekah managed to keep her trolley hidden. Only Helen and I ever knew her secret. However, after the rituals of the final year examinations, Rebekah was offered a scholarship to the prestigious Trinity College, Cambridge whilst I became a schoolteacher. It was not surprising that we lost touch with one another as Rebekah was destined for any academic position that she wanted whilst I found happiness in the achievements of my teenaged pupils. I still met up with Helen regularly and she told me that Rebekah had "come out" and no longer hid her trolley.

Five years elapsed during which time both Helen and I bore children. My husband, another teacher, is a brilliant dad. Helen might not have been so lucky as her partner seems to spend many evenings drinking with mates in the local pub. Gayle was desperate to be a mother but, although she and Gordon went to a great deal of trouble with medical investigation, they remained childless. Helen wondered whether it was Gayle whose insides had never recovered from the electric shock received from Rebekah. I suppose we will never know.

Helen and I met after Rebekah became an unwanted centre of attention when she said she was not really a woman, more a trolley! She proclaimed this with more than a hint of irony at a festival that claimed it was celebrating the achievements of "lesbian, gay, bisexual, transexual, queer and other gendered people". I read in the newspaper report that the organiser had shouted at her:

"We know you are a cis woman. You were a woman at birth and have never identified as anything else."

"Yes," she replied, "but I am told I am a TERF because – although I have no womb nor any physical elements that usually show that I am a woman – I am unclear whether I can ever shake off the fact that I am female. So perhaps you need to add "trolley" as one of the other genders."

I did not know what a TERF was, so Rebekah explained it when Helen and I arranged to meet her in London after the event. She said it stood for transgender-exclusionary radical feminists which did not really help me. "Why did you go to the festival?" I asked. Rebekah thought for a moment.

A tiny tear dripped from her right eye as she said: "So many of the women I have met at these events are amongst the most intelligent, sensitive, and loyal friends that anyone could have. But the sheer amount of time, energy, anger, and anxiety generated over worrying about how a tiny number of people identify themselves in relation to their sex peeves me no end. If they could focus just a tiny amount of that attention onto issues of far greater importance, many more people would be helped through their lives. Instead, I can see far right media owners clapping their hands with glee as they watch their natural opponents tearing into each other."

And with that, she reached down under her long dress and brought out a couple of beautifully wrapped parcels. Handing them to Helen and me, she said: "I cannot have kids, but I am so glad that you have them. So, you can tell them that these are gifts from an old Trolley."

THE BREATH OF THE DRAGON

Genesis 15, verses 19 – 21.

"The Kenites, and the Kenizzites, and the Kadmonites, and the Hittites, and the Perizzites, and the Rephaims, and the Amorites, and the Canaanites, and the Girgashites, and the Jebusites."

It is ironic that my father's life work of bringing the culture of the Himalayan Dragon People to the World may, itself, cause the end of this ancient culture. All those who have read the various popular classics about my father already know the extraordinary series of events that gave him access to this jealously protected community. The plane crash from which he alone emerged, the Dragon People's adoption of this 10-year-old boy as a prophetically foretold messenger, and his upbringing during which he became fluent in their language Cando which seems to have no linguistic nor etymological connections with any other known tongue. When he was twenty-five, the Dragon People brought him down from their high plateau and sent him out as a divine messenger – as they were required to do by their own ritualized law. Tradition has it that he was only the second man to have been recognised as a divine messenger in fifteen thousand years: no-one else has ever left the community.

Cando is not a written language and so recording the immense, constantly evolving work that includes the myths, history, customs, rituals and law of the Dragon People could only be undertaken by my father. The fate of the anthropological expedition that attempted to contact the community soon after my father's re-emergence as a young man was the same as that of various travellers who have inadvertently strayed in their search for an easy route between Europe, India and China. The local lowland communities have learnt how to assuage the Dragon and have long since given up thoughts of militant opposition. The Dragon People have dominated the region at a distance through fear, tradition and their discovery of how to refine a highly inflammatory oil from a tree that only grows at the altitude that they inhabit. The oil (ouzo) serves as fuel, the basis for cooking, a medical (and hallucinogenic) inhalant – and as the ammunition for a kind of flame-thrower against which the lowlanders have no defence. Every other year, at the winter solstice, one of the lowland villages takes their turn in giving a young girl to the Dragon as their peace offering. The Dragon (in reality, two men covered in animal hides holding a flame-thrower) escort the terrified girl up the mountain where she joins the harem of other women from the lowlands. The harem does not speak Cando: but it does appear to have protected the Dragon People from falling foul of the greatest danger for so isolated a community – inbreeding.

My father's various best-sellers about the Dragon People have financed his great work, writing down the text of 'The Breath of the Dragon'. His first book, arguing against the sending of the first expedition, foretold the cost of such an exploit. 'The bill from the hill' only made a major impact after the expedition was lost. The next book, arguing that the culture of the Dragon People should never be seen as inferior to the more popular cultures outside, topped the best-sellers list for over a year. 'Anything you can do, they Cando better' effectively gave my father complete financial independence. It was only then that he left my mother and me and returned, alone, to his People – a divine messenger with a mission.

Just before he died, my father paid for the 50-volume, 2,000,000-word text of 'The Breath of the Dragon', to be published. Twice as long as the Bible, its roots go back further than any comparable work, but there are no signs of influence on the Vedic lore and only some passing similarities to Buddhist beliefs (which should put an end to the stupid speculation that Siddartha Gautama – the Buddha – was the only other messenger from the Dragon). Once scholars and admirers of my father's dedication have had time to read this vast work, I think that there will be a reassessment of our relationship with this proud community, and 'The Breath of the Dragon' will take its rightful place in World literature. Composed and recited under the influence of oozo, the work is consistent, incoherent drivel. I suspect that the community will not long survive the Sino-Japanese, armed expedition that is now filming life on the plateau. The Dragon People's certain extinction will be welcomed by their lowland neighbours and, if anyone bothers to wade through my father's transcriptions, regretted by nobody.

RECLUSE

Professor Carl Magnusson was famously reclusive. He had also solved some of the most intractable problems of mathematics by an astonishing and elegant recombination of widely differing disciplines.

The professor never taught undergraduates. Immersed in his research, there was never time to give to the younger generation. As a student in Life Sciences, Loren Singh was surprised and excited when her Director of Studies said she was to go to Carl Magnusson for tuition.

She gingerly opened the study door and sat before the professor.

"I understand that you are to be one of the team chosen to study the essential elements of life," Magnusson announced to her.

This was news to Loren, but she assumed that the professor had foreknowledge of many decisions being made in the upper echelons of the ancient University.

"Do you feel prepared to tackle some of the questions that your colleagues will have not been able to answer?"

Loren hesitated. This sounded like a question that could only be answered affirmatively if she wanted to continue learning with Magnusson. But her instinctive response was always to tell the truth as to how she felt. She had realised, despite her youth, that dissembling rarely worked outside the realms of politics and criminal activity. So, she said that she did not know whether she was ready but would be keen to attempt with others to get to grips with what needed to be explained.

Magnusson seemed happy with this tactful response. After a few seconds, he asked what sounded like an initiation question.

"Can you tell me what defines life?"

She knew this was one of the first questions programmers working in artificial intelligence were set. She had learnt their definitions but was unsure whether the brilliant professor would necessarily agree with them.

"Well, the capacity to reproduce seems to be critical," she began. "And higher life forms all seem to have the ability to communicate."

Magnusson interjected. "So, as mycelia reproduce and communicate chemically with all other vegetable and animal life forms that surround fungi, would you class a mycelium as a higher life form?"

She thought for a moment. Then went one; "just because they can reproduce and communicate, maybe that is not sufficient for them to be defined as a higher life form. Perhaps more is required. But they are certainly a life form."

"I have set the same question to my family of Magnussons in China, France and Brazil," the professor admitted. "And they have been unable to identify what more is required. One or two even question the centrality of the reproductive process. But if you and the team you are joining can come up with a satisfactory answer, we would be glad to hear it."

The silence indicated to Loren that this initial tutorial was finished. She had been set a task and needed to join the embryonic team organised to answer the professor's question.

As she rose to leave, he said "The university is annoyed at the amount of electrical energy I am consuming so could you please switch me off as you leave?"

JUDAH

Judah left the hotel after a late breakfast. He had been up into the early hours doing business with other traders he had known for years: making small gains in small deals and losing in cards. He made his way across town where he had a lunch appointment with Johnny. He was not looking forward to this ordeal. He had to be careful with his food – not that he cared about being kosher, or anything like that. It was his grumbling ulcer that needed nursing through the day, and the place that Johnny insisted where they eat had a cook who was probably paid commission on the quantity of lard consumed. Still, you did not argue with Johnny. Everyone knew that he was a small-time crook, but he had friends who enjoyed any excuse to indulge in a little playful violence. Judah only traded with Johnny if he really had to. Johnny liked to bully him, and Judah used their occasional meetings to glean information about who else he should avoid.

After lunch, Judah retired for a long session in the lavatory whilst Johnny went home. On his way, Johnny bumped into his brother, Robert. Now if Johnny was bad, Robert was worse. They walked into the nearest bar to have a few whiskies as they had not seen each other for two days. Robert wanted to tell Johnny about his latest venture: an extortion racket involving video hire. Johnny said he thought it sounded "great": but he used the same description for all Robert's business activities – and meant it. In the corner of the bar sat Sergeant Potts. He watched the brothers – he always did. They knew he was there – they always did. He had observed Judah and Johnny at lunch also. He suspected Judah of being the "Jewish brains" behind the brothers' criminal activities.

He knew he would never be able to pin anything on Judah. "Here today, gone tomorrow," he told the young constable about the trader. "He's far too smart to leave any trace of his orders. He just arrives, tells them what to do and disappears, so he is never around when the crimes are committed." Constable Stevens had never seen Judah, but he knew the shopkeepers who were frightened of Robert. To tell the truth, he was a bit afraid of Robert. Even at school he had avoided Robert: although he was sometimes hard to dodge when he came at you for not sharing your pocket money with his kid brother, Johnny. Constable Stevens was on duty that afternoon when he saw Robert and Johnny leave the bar, closely followed by Sergeant Potts. He watched them leave the premises, then continued his measured walk up the hill.

The children were leaving school, so he stopped the odd car to let a few cross the road. One of the mums, Sandra, thanked him with a smile. He had always had a strong fancy towards Sandra – ever since he had rescued her little kitten from a tree when she was 13 years old. But she had fallen for Tom, the only motor mechanic whom Sergeant Potts would ever use. Tom was a bit older than Sandra and, as chance would have it, drove up in a customer's car. He leaned out of the window and spoke to his wife. Sandra nodded enthusiastically and Tom drove off. When he got back to the garage, he reported that the car was in perfect working order and turned to service the last vehicle for the afternoon. It was an old van that Tom disliked. It was badly designed, and he needed to remove whole sections of the engine just to replace one worn part. It was time-consuming, unrewarding work compared to the repairs he often did on the wealthy customers' saloon or sports cars. When he finally finished, he knocked off for the day – driving home to Sandra in the car he had built himself. He passed the police station where Potts and Stevens were just finishing their shift. He passed Robert and Johnny, who had got together for a quick, evening tour of video shops before retiring home.

Only Judah was not to be seen as he wandered far away. He would not come home for many years yet.

THE BRIDGES

Ysau and Yakob Del Ponte were always fighting. Ysau, the older brother, was studious and found Yakob's delight in making mischief annoying. Yakob, who was taller and stronger than Ysau even before they were teenagers, found Ysau's serious nature a perfect target for his pranks. Their father, Yzaak, the much-respected owner of the Del Ponte bus company, always knew that Ysau had to inherit the business – and after the young man had qualified as an accountant, he soon became acquainted with all the financial details of the family firm.

Yakob, however, showed no interest in mechanised road transport. On the contrary, his great passion was cycling. He joined the State Cycling Club whilst still at school and after intensive training distinguished himself by winning the State Championship. His ability to leave the peloton behind at an early stage of the race defined him as an individualist who, nonetheless, was a popular figure amongst fellow cyclists. His prowess at sports was not confined to racing. Every weekend he could be seen hang-gliding from the nearby peaks and, after sailing about the skies for half an hour, landing gently on the beach amongst bemused sun seekers.

It was whilst participating in an international hang-gliding event that Yakob met the equally fit Yisrael. Yisrael's love of the air had extended to building and operating airships. These great monsters would rise over his home city carrying hundreds of passengers across the desert to the coast. The ticket price was half of that charged by the competing airline and, although the flight took longer, many holidaymakers preferred the relaxed journey to the airport queues and cramped conditions aboard the jets. Instead of just hang-gliding over the shore at home, Yakob imagined flying an airship across the bay to link the twin cities on either bank without getting caught up in the crowded traffic of the Ponte Sagrada. He chatted to Yisrael about the possibility and was excited to find his close friend more than willing to give it a trial.

Although the usual bureaucracy delayed the initial flight by over a year, the airship service across the bay proved a tremendous success. Two airships were deployed criss-crossing the bay every half an hour. Yakob followed this success by gaining victory in the national cycling championship that imprinted his face across the media as firmly as the launch of the airship service had done. As a household name, Yakob should have been the pride of his family but instead, the childhood feuding with Ysau was now taking a more adult and sinister form. The success of the airship service had made a serious dent in the profitability of the family bus company. Thousands now preferred floating leisurely across the bay to the noisy trip over the enormous Ponte Sagrada by bus. Ysau, now in charge of the company, wrote to his brother asking him to close the airship service down as a mark of respect for their father whose firm was now suffering because of Yakob's experiment. Yakob, aware of the effort that he and Yisrael had put into getting the service running and its subsequent popularity with commuters, refused.

We now come to the murkiest part of the story. Perhaps no one will ever know the truth of what happened. Ysau always denied having anything to do with the fire that destroyed the airship station and one of the craft that was parked there overnight. The police investigation concluded that the culprit might have been an off-target firework that had exploded near gas canisters instead of high in the sky during the Carnival celebrations. Yisrael, never wanting to stand between the brothers, wondered whether the annoyance felt by Ysau had led to one of his over-enthusiastic employees taking matters into their own hands without their master's permission. But Yakob was more suspicious and could not believe his brother's declarations of innocence. The gulf between the brothers was now so wide that nothing seemed able to bridge it.

The airship service never resumed. The City authorities decided that this means of transport was too dangerous to continue. The risk assessment was carried out by a firm on whose Board Ysau sat – which seemed to confirm Yakob's belief that the entire demise of the airship enterprise was down to his brother's jealousy. Yakob took his fury out on the road by cycling with a fervour that could not be matched by any of his fellow cyclists. He would speed around the roads, overtaking cars and buses on the outside lane, and, on occasion, even outpacing the chasing motorbike rider and photographer employed by the newspapers to take his picture. One weekend, he calmed down long enough to rejoin the following peloton. Since he spent most of his time riding far ahead of the others, he had not noticed how the Club had expanded following his success. Instead of a few dozen, there were now several hundred men and women riding together wanting to emulate their hero, Yakob. Talking with them, he discovered that most worked across the Ponte Sagrada and only had time to take serious exercise in the weekends on their bikes. By the following weekend, Yakob had devised a new strategy to replace what he and Yisrael had lost.

Publicity for his national health campaign succeeded in attracting the support of government and health-related corporations without arousing the suspicion of Ysau. But when he followed this up with his 'Cycling to Work' project, his proposal to set aside a lane on the Bridge specifically for cyclists caused a furore. His day of action when thousands of cyclists rode over the Ponte Sagrada using all the lanes as a protest "to end discrimination against health" led to the authorities caving in to his demands. Once again, the profitability of the bus company was hit by the defection of its passengers. Yakob set up giant cycle parks with toilet and shower facilities on both sides of the Bridge and started a lucrative business in cycle repair and hire. Ysau did not bother to ask his brother to desist. He knew that this popular pastime now had the backing of government and the public as a way of combining open-air exercise with getting to work in the pleasant company of other riders. Yakob would often accompany what he described as his pelotons across the Bridge. Unlike the fragile infrastructure underpinning the airship venture, nothing appeared to stand in the way of the continuing success in this new enterprise.

Ysau had inherited his father's head for figures. He knew exactly the number of buses required to provide a profitable service, how many drivers he needed to employ, how much fuel he would be advised to purchase in advance and how much it would cost to retain the support of officials and politicians. He carried this sort of data around in his head and was able to negotiate deals quickly without recourse to notes, computers and calculators. He was a talented accountant with an expert knowledge in his field. He was a faithful husband and devoted father to his children – a model family man and pillar of the community. The only matter that had upset him was his brother's venture into airship competition. His frustrated expression of anger at Yakob's venture was intensified as it impacted upon the bus service but, in truth, the drop in profits was less of an issue than the increasingly non-quantifiable effect that left him unsure of his figures. He hated uncertainty.

Although Ysau had always regarded Yakob as something of a show-off, he did feel genuinely happy when his younger brother became the national cycling champion. "I just wish he would stick to cycling and not try his hand at running the airship service. I would do anything to see that venture closed down so I could get back to the regular pattern of bus service scheduling and budgeting," he was heard to say. After the fire, and in his darker moments, Ysau wondered if Yisrael was right in suspecting that a bus company employee, anxious to gain favour with the boss, might have gone too far.

Perhaps he himself was partly to blame for expressing his frustrations so openly. He would never know but carried a hidden burden of guilt that he dared not express.

When the pelotons became a regular feature on the Bridge, Ysau was careful not to say anything that could be construed as antagonistic to the popular Yakob and his followers. He even gave written instructions to all his drivers to be especially courteous towards the cyclists. Yakob heard about this and was puzzled by his brother's solicitude. The drivers took it upon themselves to use only the lane furthest from the one designated for the cyclists. So, motorists frequently found themselves channelled between a long line of slow-moving buses and huge bunches of enthusiastic cyclists. Local car drivers do not always stick strictly to the rules of the road. However, any filmed trespassing onto the cycle lane were invariably stopped and fined by the police as they left the Bridge. Soon the Bridge became known as the best disciplined road in the country.

The Ponte Sagrada itself represents a major feat of civil engineering. Nine miles long and stretching from one city to the other, it climbs to an unusual height at its centre to allow the passage of oil rigs into and out of the bay. The night of the great storm saw traffic gradually leave the roads. The Bridge was practically deserted when the disaster happened. Blown from its moorings by the sheer force of the wind and rain, the massive oil rig picked up speed as it headed out into the bay. Out of control, it rammed one of the central piers of the Bridge with such force that the foundation of the pier cracked. The rig rebounded and was blown into the pier again and again. Eventually the rig caught fire and sank against the damaged Bridge section. The Ponte Sagrada was closed and on the following day, as the storm showed no sign of abating, large cracks appeared across the damaged sections. By the evening the first blocks of roadway began falling into the water and within two days an entire road section had dissolved together with the broken pier.

With no way for buses nor bicycles to cross the bay, Ysau made a move to bridge the gap between himself and his brother. Visiting him the day after the storm had subsided, he made his proposal and asked Yakob to consider it carefully. That night Yakob slept badly as he turned over Ysau's idea in his head again and again. He could see no flaws in the plan but still harboured suspicions about his brother's motives. Perhaps this was a fraternal but unwritten admission of guilt for past misdeeds. But then Yakob thought about how the peletons and buses had come to share the Bridge without any problem – indeed, with Ysau's express orders to ensure that the cyclists were treated with care. Yakob, ever impetuous, decided the next morning to accept Ysau's offer.

And so Ysau purchased two out-of-commission catamarans and had them running passengers between the shores within a week. The boats, named Yakob One and Yakob Two, carried only foot passengers but were an instant success as there was no alternative available for desperate commuters. Two months later, the two giant ferries – named Yakob Three and Yakob Four – were in operation carrying cars and lorries as well as pedestrians. Yakob headed the marketing and presentation of the new service whilst Ysau handled the finances. The jointly held company was the first time that the two brothers had worked together ... ever! Yet they seemed to catch the public mood better than when they worked apart. Once repaired, with ceremonial rituals and pageantry, the Ponte Sagrada was reopened. It carried buses and pelotons again, yet the ferries remained the most popular, relaxed and (for motorists) the cheapest form of transport across the bay.

Yakob One and Yakob Two were retired at the same time as many of Ysau's ageing buses, inherited from his father's time. In an unprecedented show of brotherly love, Yakob bought Ysau a couple of brand-new coaches so that he could continue the Del Ponte business. In return, Ysau bought Yakob a pair of luxury airships.

Finally, Yisrael and Yakob went off on their preordained mission to operate the new aerial service ... but far, far away from the Ponte Sagrada, the Sacred Bridge.

INDEX OF STORIES

Book 1   **THE TZADIK**

- 42   Robinson
- 47   Odyssey
- 60   Tristan & Isolde

Book 2   **BRAZILIAN TALES**

- 80   Flora
- 97   Monologue
- 101   Regret
- 102   Scoop
- 105   The clichés of life
- 108   The Cloudmaker

Book 3   **TALES FROM NOWHERE**

- 121   To see the sea
- 127   The compendium of pain
- 130   Trans
- 133   Kwame
- 140   The tree in the park
- 142   The Tailors
- 149   Streets ahead
- 150   Red Handed
- 156   Gline
- 161   Dream Viewers
- 166   Convict colony
- 168   Cheshire cat
- 169   It's a wise man who knows his father

Book 4   INTERLUDE

174 Friendship lost
188 The Teiresias dilemma

Book 5   GREEK HOLIDAY

203 The Pithos
206 Sirens
210 Drowned
213 The Island Rape
229 Lucky Luke

Book 6   MORE JEWISH TALES UNTOLD

235 Ezra and Nehemiah
238 Pinchbec
245 Intifada
248 The Interview
249 Grave Injustice
252 The Hunt
253 Death in the family
256 At the crossroads
258 Trolley
268 The Breath of the Dragon
271 Recluse
273 Judah
276 The Bridges

www.ingramcontent.com/pod-product-compliance
Lightning Source LLC
Chambersburg PA
CBHW051544010526
44118CB00022B/2567